YOU CAN TRAIN YOUR HORSE TO DO
ANYTHING!

On Target™ Training: Clicker Training and Beyond

Also by Shawna and Vinton Karrasch

Video
YOU CAN TRAIN YOUR HORSE TO DO ANYTHING!: Clicker Training and Beyond

YOU CAN TRAIN YOUR HORSE TO DO
ANYTHING!

On Target™ Training: Clicker Training and Beyond

SHAWNA and VINTON KARRASCH

with ARLENE J. NEWMAN

Foreword by JOHN MADDEN

KENILWORTH PRESS

First published in 2000 by
Kenilworth Press Ltd
Addington
Buckingham
MK18 2JR

Co-published simultaneously in the United States of America by Trafalgar Square
Publishing, North Pomfret, Vermont 05053

Disclaimer of Liability
The authors and publishers shall have neither liability nor responsibility to any person
or entity with respect to any loss or damage caused or alleged to be caused directly or
indirectly by the information contained in this book. While the book is as accurate of
the authors can make it, there may be errors, omissions, and inaccuracies.

British Library Cataloguing in Publication Data
A CIP record for this book is available from the British Library

ISBN 1–872119–27–1

Jacket and book design by Carrie Fradkin

Colour separation by Tenon & Polert Colour Scanning Ltd

Printed and bound in Hong Kong

Dedication

We dedicate this book to our horses, whom we love dearly. They are the pilots for On Target Training, guiding the way and continuing to teach us on a daily basis. Though they will not live forever, hopefully the lessons they teach us will endure.

Thank you Brewster, Dandy, George, Hershey, and Mint.

Table of Contents

A Note to Readers Outside the USA

When you begin reading this book it will be clear to you that we live in America. We have used American terminology, which sometimes differs to that used in Britain and other English-speaking countries. We are confident that you will understand our meaning, but please keep in mind these three equivalent terms as they come up repeatedly in the text: halter = headcollar, barn = stable, and stall = box.

The Authors

Acknowledgments

Starting a new business can be quite difficult. Especially when you're trying to introduce a new concept to the equine industry—an industry steeped in tradition. This book is the culmination of this huge but rewarding undertaking. With the guidance and support of a few key figures we have been able to weather the storms as well as enjoy the successes. We could not have come to this juncture in our lives without the influence of these people.

The first person to believe in our ideas was Susan Karrasch. Her belief in us has never wavered. She has kept us both grounded and optimistic, even when things got really tough. She is truly exceptional.

The first equine professional to get behind us was John Madden. He had the foresight to see the potential of clicker and target training before we had ever applied our concepts to horses. He, along with wife Beezie, gave us our leg up in the horse industry. They are great horsemen who have taught us a tremendous amount and given us once-in-a-lifetime opportunities.

Another important influence has been Trafalgar Square Publishing. We signed on with Trafalgar when our business was in its infancy. They had faith in our potential and took a chance with us. Our publisher Caroline Robbins has been a great help in editing our work and making it clear for our readers. Martha Cook, particularly, has been a great source of advice and guidance. We are quite proud to be part of the Trafalgar family.

We would also like to acknowledge: Arlene Newman for helping us put our work on paper; Sally Brown and Buck Hazeldine who have always been there for us (and our horses); Dan Kramer, for whom we have tremendous respect and appreciation; John and Renie Poole, who help us to keep objective; Lynn and Allan Schriver, who help to give us peace of mind whether we're at home or on the road; and the countless people who've taken the time to send letters, e-mails, or messages telling us of their successes. Thank you to all who have helped us get to this point in our lives.

Foreword

*I*t is often said that there's nothing new in the equestrian arts—no silver bullet, no magic pill. But can we achieve our training goals by improving our methods? Certainly! I believe in classic horsemanship. I'm a traditionalist—I always have been and always will be. Traditionally, equine training has been based on the application and removal of adversives—leg, hand, seat, bit, spur, stick. These are all aids that, when applied and then removed, yield appropriate behavior. In my experience, even within this classical system, the most successful riders and trainers incorporate reward in their training, whether consciously or unconsciously.

In this text, Vinton and Shawna Karrasch share with their readers what the most successful riders and trainers have always understood, albeit at times unconsciously, the importance of reward. With their explanation of the On Target Training system, they have elevated the use of reward to conscious thought and provided a workable method for its systematic implementation.

In my world of competitive show jumping, communication between partners, horse and rider, is the most essential ingredient. On many occasions in training our horses we have used positive reinforcement to get by a particularly rough spot, especially if the horse has developed defenses from past training. By employing the On Target system, we are able to express clearly to the horse exactly what it has done well and when. This system has had a great effect on my training methods even beyond the use of a clicker or a target. The underlying philosophies of setting the horse up to succeed, considering and working on motivation, and rewarding the good while ignoring (if possible) the bad, has affected my own work profoundly.

Shawna and Vinton make an important contribution to horse training with this book. Whether taken in whole or even in part, every serious horseman must consider and understand the On Target Training system. Its methods and, even more importantly, the fundamentals of this system, should not be ignored. Regardless of one's experience, background, or equine discipline, this book is an education for everyone who cares about horses.

John Madden
Owner and trainer of John Madden Sales, Inc.,
he and wife Beezie specialize in developing horses and riders for top-level show jumping competition.

Introduction

Vinton and I met under the most ironic of circumstances. I was successfully immersed in my career as a trainer of marine mammals at Sea World in San Diego, California, and just beginning to learn the rudiments of riding and horse training. Vinton had been a successful high-level competitor and trainer of show jumpers and had come to Sea World to pursue a career as a trainer of marine mammals. That meeting dramatically changed our lives, both personally and professionally. Ultimately, we became partners in business and in marriage. The result of our shared experiences and ideas about how horses learn and can be better motivated became the basis for the On Target Training system.

While I now derive tremendous satisfaction from my work with horses, during my childhood I never imagined my future would involve such a pursuit. My earliest exposure to horses did little to pique my interest. My grandfather had some Quarter Horses on his farm and any visitors could ride them, assuming they could find and catch them. These horses had their run of the farm, along with the cattle. They were tolerant of people and put up with the grandchildren, but they didn't seem to have much personality or spirit. In fact, they didn't seem to enjoy their interactions with people very much at all. Because of these early experiences, I couldn't understand what some of my friends found so fascinating about riding. Instead, I became interested in exotic animals, which eventually led to my career at Sea World.

Here is Vinton, 18 years old, just three years after he started riding. He is competing at the North American Young Rider Show Jumping Championships in 1988.

My perspective on horses changed, however, when I was invited to a grand-prix jumping event by one of the owners of Sea World. She was in San Diego to help coordinate a horse show at nearby Del Mar, and invited several Sea World trainers to attend the show jumping event that evening. This was an aspect of riding I had never before seen, and I was quite intrigued. After watching the competition that night, I decided to learn how to ride and began finding out more about horses and horse training. To my amazement, I learned that the system we trained animals with at Sea World was not used to train horses. When I asked why, no one offered what I found to be a valid reason.

Thinking that horses may have to be trained differently than marine mammals, I set out to learn how horses were traditionally trained. I started taking riding lessons with Marion Hadden at Rancho Riding Club, Rancho Santa Fe, California. From my first lesson, I was hooked, and soon afterward, I bought my first horse. One of the first things I noticed as a new rider was how many problems people encountered with their horses and that these problems were regarded as routine. I observed this common dilemma when I rode at shows and attended clinics. For example, I saw horses who had bad manners, avoided people, and seemed uncomfortable and discontented. With my background as an animal behaviorist, I saw easy solutions for these problems. The reward-reinforcement system we used at Sea World had already been proven to be safe, easy, and highly effective. It was also the only training system I knew. However, I was not then thinking about changing the traditional horse training system. I was focused on learning more about it.

While I was immersing myself in the horse world, Vinton was putting closure on his career as a professional rider and trainer and positioning himself to start a new career as a trainer of marine mammals. He had competed as a junior up through the grand-prix level and spent years training with some of the top professionals in the discipline of show jumping including George Morris, Anne Kursinski, Julie Winkel, Beezie Patton Madden, and John Madden. Vinton began riding at the age of 15, which was quite a late start for a serious junior rider. Nevertheless, he progressed at a fast and furious pace, studying and absorbing all he could to become a successful jumper rider. After graduating from the junior ranks, Vinton turned professional. He focused on riding and training his own up-and-coming and grand-prix jumpers as well as coaching his clients and training their horses. Vinton is a perfectionist and he found many aspects of maintaining his jumper business frustrating, particularly the effort to maintain a balance with coaching his clients, developing his horses, and managing the business itself. Ultimately, he realized he had lost perspective on what attracted him to the business in the first place, which was the horse itself. Not knowing how to reclaim his lost passion, he decided to make a clean break from the equine industry and start a different career where he could work with animals while someone else managed the business. While he was showing horses on the Florida circuit, Vinton had seen performances at Sea World and recognized the high level of training and communication during those performances. He became interested in training marine mammals at Sea World.

Vinton started working at Sea World, waiting for a position to become available in the Animal Training Department. He had given up his horse business and sold everything he owned related to it including his horses, trailer, and equipment. One day after I had just finished a riding lesson, a mutual friend who knew we both worked at Sea World and liked horses introduced us. Amazingly, Vinton had been riding some horses for fun at the same barn where I took lessons. We had both been working and riding at the same places!

In October of 1994, Vinton and I began the discussion that eventually led to our system while driving to watch a grand-prix jumping event at Flintridge Riding Club near Los Angeles. At the time, I didn't know Vinton very well and he struck me as a rather quiet person. I anticipated that this two-hour drive would be filled with my chatter, but I was completely wrong. Vinton and I had a conversation that had a profound effect on both of our lives. I was learning about horses and horse training and was told by the experienced horse people I talked to that it didn't seem likely that the system used to train marine mammals would work with horses. I was certain the system would work for horses but thought I first needed to learn much more about the current system that had been successfully in use for hundreds of years.

Vinton and I started talking about how horses are trained. He listened with an open mind. I asked him why the tried and true system used at Sea World to train animals wasn't used with horses. He was the first horse person to take my question seriously and to consider the possibility of training horses differently. He began presenting scenarios to me, asking me how I would use reward-reinforcement to solve various problems and teach specific behaviors. One of the questions he asked was how I would feed or reinforce when working a horse under saddle. I explained that I might have to use the rein to gently pull his head to the side. Then, I would lean forward and feed him. Vinton asked me how I would apply reward-reinforcement to training flying lead changes. At the time, I didn't know how to train a horse to do a flying change, so Vinton told me the usual steps. I explained how I would use reward-reinforcement for each step of the training process. It made sense to both of us.

In this conversation, we talked quite a bit about jumping style. How a horse jumps was of particular interest to Vinton since the form in which a horse jumps can make the difference between a horse worth $5,000 and a horse worth $100,000. At Sea World, jumping is what we would refer to as an aerial behavior. With marine mammals these include bows (when the dolphins jump out of the water and enter headfirst), breeches (when the dolphins jump and land on their sides), back flips, and high jumps (when they jump and touch a target). The beginning steps for teaching these maneuvers are quite different than the finished product, but by using behavioral principles, trainers can change the performance as they desire. The same concept can be applied to teaching horses to jump. Naturally, horses vary in their athletic ability, but much can be done to teach a horse how to use himself more efficiently. We talked further and Vinton's interest really grew, especially when we talked about using this system to improve attitude. No matter which species of animal you work with, a good attitude is paramount for progress, safety, and results. We had several follow-up conversations in which we talked in detail about how reward-reinforcement could be applied to horse training, which convinced Vinton the system could work for horses.

Soon afterward, we had the chance to talk with John Madden, who was in the area to design jumping courses for a show in Del Mar. Vinton and John were friends, and we made plans to get together for dinner. During the visit, Vinton talked with John about our thoughts on incorporating reward-reinforcement in the training process. John listened carefully. He was interested in anything that could improve a horse's motivation or performance. He went home to New York with a clicker and planned to try it out on one of the horses ridden by Beezie Patton Madden, who frequently represents the U.S. Equestrian Team in international competition.

A few days after John got home, he called to let us know how well reward-reinforcement was working. He was surprised at how responsive the horse was and how quickly he understood what John was teaching him. John invited us to spend a week working with the horses at his barn. We eagerly took him up on the invitation. This was the first time we would apply the principles of training I used with marine mammals to horses. This was the beginning of the On Target Training system.

After a week, it was clear that the system we were developing based on reward-reinforcement worked well. The horses were quick learners. Vinton, John, and I decided to move ahead and try this on a full-time basis, so in January of 1996, Vinton and I moved from California to Cazenovia, New York, the site of John Madden Sales Stables, to begin our work in earnest.

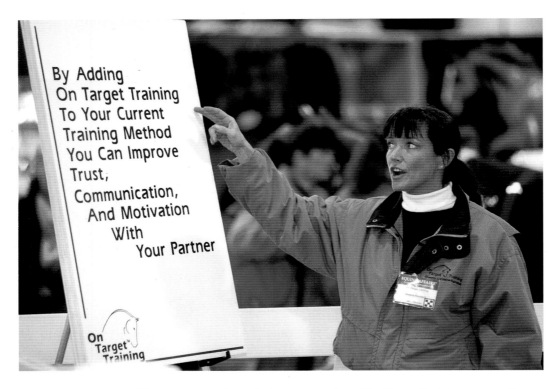

By Adding
On Target Training
To Your Current
Training Method
You Can Improve
Trust,
Communication,
And Motivation
With
Your Partner

On
Target™
Training

2 I'm teaching the basic principles of On Target Training to an audience at Equine Affaire—a horse-related exposition—held in Springfield, Massachusetts in 1999.

We couldn't have found a more ideal laboratory and proving ground for our system than John's operation, which provided us the opportunity to fine tune our system based on the wide variety of horses at his facility. John routinely imports talented show jumping prospects from Europe and South America, and finds them throughout the United States. This gave us the opportunity to work with a group of horses of diverse ages, backgrounds, and levels of experience, ranging from weanlings to Olympic contenders. We worked with seven or eight horses each day. These horses presented a variety of issues for us to undertake, from ground manners to under-saddle work. The experience was invaluable, especially for me as a newcomer to the horse world.

3   Vinton is demonstrating these principles under saddle. He is teaching Mint to do a half-pass.

Initially, Vinton was reluctant to get back into the horse business. First, he helped me by giving me the guidance I needed to train horses, but had no interest in riding himself. Soon afterward, he recognized how much he enjoyed riding when teaching horses with no pressure to compete. Riding and training horses have taken on an even greater meaning to Vinton as we have developed the On Target Training system. When we apply this system to horses, Vinton and I observe a fundamental change in the relationship between horse and rider. The horses seem happy to interact with us, the learning process accelerates, and there is much less frustration for both horse and rider.

After about a year of tailoring and honing our training system, we realized the time was right to begin reaching out to the millions of people who wanted to build better relationships with their horses. Interest in our work was growing. We had started at John and Beezie's with the intent of doing some concentrated learning. Soon afterward, people began questioning us on how to improve their horses' behavior. We recognized right away that if we wanted lasting results, we needed to teach the owners how to educate their horses. The old adage, "If you give a man a fish, you feed him for a day. If you teach him how to fish, you feed him for a lifetime," applied to our approach.

The best forum seemed to be clinics, where we could answer questions and come up with solutions to individual problems. Vinton and I have since conducted clinics for people with a wide variety of equine interests from the Minneapolis Mounted Police to the U.S. Equestrian Team's Festival of Champions in Gladstone, New Jersey. We decided to write this book after getting requests at our clinics for written material.

As an animal trainer, I have found two aspects of my career particularly satisfying. I really enjoy watching animals learn. I have always felt that the animals I work with enjoy our time together and that I have enriched their lives while teaching them something new. As you progress with the On Target Training system, you will see your horse, dog, or other animal start to blossom before your eyes. I derive just as much satisfaction from teaching the other half of the training equation, the owner or trainer. It's a pleasure to see them begin to comprehend how the system works and become eager to apply it to their training goals. We've received numerous letters, telephone calls, and e-mails from owners and trainers seeking advice and telling us their success stories using the On Target Training system.

Clinics give us the opportunity to interact more intensively with horse owners, handlers, and riders. We share our knowledge and experiences and we often are presented with new challenges, such as a horse training issue with which we are unfamiliar. As a result, Vinton and I gain an opportunity to learn. When we started offering clinics, we spoke with small groups who were unfamiliar with the concepts we teach. Now, we speak to much larger groups, and many of the participants have heard of our system through magazine articles, our video, college courses, or through word of mouth. Some are already using the On Target Training system with their horses. We prefer to teach the fundamentals of the system in a clinic format that focuses on teaching people how to train their own horses. If the owner or trainer becomes conversant with the system and follows through, the training results will last much longer than if we trained the horse ourselves and then sent him home. Sometimes, the problem that needed to be addressed in training can resurface with a change in environment. However, if horse owners know the steps to take to undo the problem, they can minimize its reoccurrence.

Vinton and I married on May 3, 1997, and began building the farm in Maryland from where we base our home and our On Target Training work. This has been an exciting, educational journey for us. While we thoroughly enjoy teaching people, we have also learned a tremendous amount ourselves and continue to do so. Each clinic and every situation is different. With each new step, we continue to grow and improve.

CHAPTER

Why On Target Training Works

Did you ever wish you could get your horse to consistently perform to the best of his ability? I have yet to meet the horse person who would not appreciate improved performance. Have you ever been faced with annoying or dangerous equine problems you would like to eliminate? I can't think of anyone who would say "no." Have you ever wanted to teach your horse, from the very beginning, positive experiences that give him motivation to succeed in performing whatever you ask of him without developing any undesirable behavior? Whether the issue that's been troubling you relates to ground manners or riding, On Target Training offers a system that's simple, logical, and scientifically proven to provide everyone who works with horses a way to eliminate objectionable behavior, start a young or green horse positively, or enhance a current training program. When you integrate our system into your program, your horse will eagerly volunteer to perform as you request.

FROM KILLER WHALES TO HORSES: HOW I LEARNED TO TRAIN ANIMALS

My interest in animals and their behavior started at an early age. I was fascinated with all kinds, especially species native to Africa. During my later childhood years in San Diego, I also enjoyed many visits to Sea World. But I didn't put my interest in animal behavior together with my fondness for all things aquatic until I took a summer course while pursuing a biology degree. The class was a field study of the finback whale and its ecosystem, held in Mexico. When I completed the course, I came home with a new perspective on my future. Following my newfound interests, I acquired a job as a tour guide and narrator in the education department at Sea World.

When I learned of an opening for the next summer in animal training, I applied right away, passed Sea World's rigorous swim test, microphone test, interview process, and was hired. My initial work there was strictly behind the scenes. I worked in the sea lion and otter area and did husbandry tasks such as preparing food and cleaning the habitats. I was also trained to do back-up support for the shows, including bringing animals to the stage areas and sending them cues from behind the stage asking them to perform various show behaviors.

My summer job developed into a full-time position. I couldn't have asked for a job more tailor-made to my interests. Not only did I have the opportunity to spend my days around animals, but, better yet, I got to interact with them, build relationships, and watch the youngsters grow and develop into show performers.

The first year of working with animals at Sea World is an apprenticeship period. You observe, learn, and concentrate on caretaking tasks. After that initial experience, you begin working with the animals and preparing them for shows. Apprentices work with the most predictable, experienced, and forgiving animals. An experienced trainer works with the apprentices teaching them about **behaviors*** (actions that animals perform in their natural environment as well as new ones that are taught them), cues (the methods used to tell the animals which behavior is being requested), **criteria** (the standards that measure whether behaviors asked for are rewarded), and basic behavioral principles. The trainees at Sea World only work with behaviors the animals already know (usually behaviors related to show performances). As the trainees build a relationship with the animals they go on to participate in the shows. The equivalent situation in the horse world might be a working student who starts her career with a professional riding the trained horses before moving on to riding green horses.

---

*The language of On Target Training is full of specialized terms that you will find in the glossary at the end of this book. These terms will be boldfaced when first introduced.

As a trainee at Sea World, I worked with Felix, a female small-clawed Asian river otter. She performed in The Sea Lion and Otter Show. She was remarkable in that she enjoyed being held like this—most otters won't tolerate this level of intimacy.

As a novice trainer you gain experience and move on to train new behaviors, eventually working with some of the younger animals, using the same principles. One of the lessons I learned early on was that every new animal I worked with brought me new learning experiences.

During the ten years I spent at Sea World working with killer whales, dolphins, sea lions, walruses, and otters, I acquired the building blocks for our On Target Training system. We had to teach marine mammals, big and small, to perform show behaviors on a consistent basis. In peak sea-

5   Later, at Sea World, I graduated to working with the killer whales. Here I am riding Corky at the Shamu Show. She was the "school horse" of the whales, and many of us learned on her because she was patient, kind, and forgiving.

son, we had up to twelve shows a day and each succeeding one had to be as good as the first. These marine animals are taught complex show behaviors solely through **reward-reinforcement**, also known in behavioral texts as **positive reinforcement.** Can you imagine a halter for controlling a 10,000-pound killer whale? Even if there were such a thing, how would you discipline such a huge creature? Obviously, that concept could not work.

Another issue we had to factor in to our work with marine mammals was safety. As horsemen know, there is a potential for danger when working with large animals. Using reward-reinforcement and the training tools

I will discuss in this book, you can create a safer working relationship between you and your horse. As a training tool, reward-reinforcement can help to eliminate feelings of frustration, which can lead to aggression in your animal partner. One of our training goals at Sea World was to eliminate aggression from the training equation. Training with reward-reinforcement increased these animals' interest and motivation to perform the behaviors we taught them. Without a doubt, we taught these animals a job, but we also taught them to enjoy performing their jobs—they seemed to take pleasure in interacting with us, too. Reward-reinforcement will have a similar beneficial effect on the horses introduced to this training system.

REWARD- VERSUS REMOVAL-REINFORCEMENT

Reward-reinforcement is called positive reinforcement in behavioral psychology texts. When you use reward-reinforcement, you motivate your

6   Scratching your horse's favorite spot is probably the most useful secondary reinforcement because you can do it anytime and anywhere— under saddle or on the ground.

7 All horses enjoy being turned out. Even though its use as a secondary reinforcement is not as immediate as "scratching," most horses can be taught that they will be rewarded with a shorter work session and prompt turnout if they perform well.

horse to repeatedly perform the correct behaviors by offering him something he enjoys in return. In our program, we usually use food as a reward since horses so commonly accept it. I have yet to come across a horse who hasn't responded to food. It has tremendous power as a **reinforcer.** Food is considered by behaviorists to be a **primary,** or **unconditioned, reinforcer** because it's necessary for survival. That's why every healthy horse finds food reinforcing. When a foal is born, the first thing he does is stand, find his mother's udder, and drink.

While food is something animals need, secondary, or conditioned, reinforcers are things animals have learned to like. A secondary, or conditioned reinforcer, can also influence the likelihood of behaviors being repeated. For horses, secondary reinforcers can vary quite a bit. Some horses enjoy tactile stimuli such as being rubbed, touched, and stroked. Others don't like these feelings or seem indifferent to touch. Some horses

8 Not all horses enjoy playing with "toys." But for the ones who do, bring them their balls, cones, or whatever they like after a good lesson.

relish their turnout time and enjoy playing with balls or cones. As you get to know your horse's likes and dislikes, you will learn what your horse enjoys as a secondary, or conditioned, reinforcer.

Another way that behavior is shaped—perhaps the most prevalent method of traditional horse training—is through **removal-reinforcement,** a method we use less in our On Target Training system because it's been shown that it is not anywhere near as useful as reward-reinforcement. Psychology texts refer to removal-reinforcement as *negative* reinforcement. Most people I talk to assume negative reinforcement means **punishment.**

This is not the case at all. In this context the word "negative" is used to mean "minus" i.e. you subtract a stimulus. (On the other hand, the word "positive" refers to the addition of a stimulus.) Here is Charles Ferster and Stuart Culbertson's textbook definition out of *Behavior Principles*: "Negative reinforcement refers to an **operant performance** whose frequency increases because it has terminated an **aversive** stimulus. Both negative and positive reinforcement (reward-reinforcement) increase the frequency of a performance. In the case of negative reinforcement, the increase comes about because of the *termination* of the stimulus, while in the case of positive reinforcement, the increase occurs as a result of the *presentation* of a reinforcing stimulus."

By removing, or subtracting, an aversive stimulus, you reinforce certain behavior. Let's think about how you use a bridle when you ride. When you tighten the reins, the horse slows down or stops. In response, you soften the pressure applied to the mouth. By removing the pressure on the mouth, you reinforce the horse's correct response. The next time the horse feels this pressure, he is likely to slow down again. Using the leg to ask the horse to move forward is another example of removal-reinforcement. When you teach the horse to move forward, you apply pressure from the leg. When the horse responds correctly to the leg pressure, you soften it. Both of these common horse-training methods are classic examples of removal-reinforcement. In both instances, the reinforcement of the response is the removal of pressure. Removal-reinforcement is not a bad thing—it can be a highly effective training tool when used correctly.

Using a longe whip or rope in training programs such as round pen work is another example. As long as the horse moves forward when asked, the longe whip or rope is kept away, therefore reinforcing the desired behavior. If the horse doesn't move forward, the whip or rope may be waved in the horse's direction or touch him until he responds by moving forward, allowing the trainer to then remove the aversive.

Here is an additional example of removal-reinforcement that does not work to the trainer's advantage. Think about the horse who doesn't want his ears touched. What does he do? He lifts his head or moves it around so you can't reach his ears easily with your hand (photo 9). You may find my explanation here surprising. The horse is actually reinforcing his own behavior. He lifts his head away from your hand and the aversive, your hand, is avoided. When he does this, you can't touch his ears and his head raising and/or shaking behavior is immediately reinforced. (In Chapter

9 Hershey is avoiding me. I want to touch his ears but he has learned that by raising his head high, his ears will be out of my reach. This is a perfect example of a horse rewarding himself with his own action—a situation that should never be encouraged. If I could reach his ears, I would be able to touch them, click, and reinforce him with food—something I need to do to make progress with his reinforcement training.

Two, we'll discuss how to change the horse's response so he'll calmly accept his ears being touched.)

Behaviorists have proven that when people or animals are taught through removal-reinforcement, compliance will be minimal. In most cases, the subject will put forth only as much effort as necessary to avoid the aversive. However, when people or animals are taught using reward-reinforcement, results are stellar. This is because they are working for something they desire. With our On Target Training system, you will be

10 It's obvious that I was enjoying my work here. It seemed to me that Corky also enjoyed her performances and had great fun, too.

using reward-reinforcement to shape your horse's behavior. You'll find that your horse will keep trying harder.

You don't have to completely change your existing training program to use On Target Training. You can add reward-reinforcement to your current regimen to get better, quicker results, and increased motivation. With our system, horses seem to become more involved in the training process and in trying to figure out what they're being asked to do. This is because there is something in it for them. In fact, horses actually seem to look forward to training sessions with reward-reinforcement.

DEVELOPING "HEART" WITH ON TARGET TRAINING

I was just beginning to learn about training horses when Vinton first told me about the concept of "heart" and that all the best horses have this desirable attribute. Since I was unfamiliar with the term "heart," he explained. He told me "heart" had to do with willingness, trying, wanting to please. Mostly, as I understood it, he was describing a cooperative attitude that demonstrated exactly what we taught the animals at Sea World. The marine mammals have to like what they're doing. If they don't, they're not going to perform reliably and might cause their trainers serious injury. Coercion is not an option, so trainers have to cultivate a good attitude when they interact with animals—they need to teach them to channel their energy into their performance, not use it in an unproductive way.

I've seen a lot of horses channel their energy toward nervousness, or worse, resistance. A fundamental difference between the results of reward-reinforcement and removal-reinforcement lies in the question of training the animal's attitude. I would say most of the marine mammals I worked with were taught to have "heart" with reward-reinforcement. Yet, currently in the horse world, "heart" is regarded as a lucky fluke, not something that can be developed.

On Target Training addresses this gap in training methods. You can train your horse to have heart. Slow down and pay attention to the kind of attitudes I mentioned earlier that lend to "heart." Think about the previous discussion of removal-reinforcement versus reward-reinforcement. Removal-reinforcement gets minimal compliance while reward-reinforcement brings about remarkable results. Animals try harder for reward-reinforcement. When you see your horse exhibit the attitude you want, reinforce him. Later in the chapter, I'll show you how to accomplish this important step with your horse.

I should point out that our own horses were not the brightest, bravest, or most focused horses we have trained. They did not have the best attitudes. When we started working with them, they were in fact, the two worst horses in our program. Mint was a two-year-old when we met him and clearly a quitter. He wouldn't try hard at all. In fact, he would shut down or walk away even when all we were doing was basic training. George was a rather precocious weanling with a minimal attention span. I reinforced Mint for trying, while George got reinforced for concentrating. Since we bought the horses from John Madden and have continued to spend time working with them, no one, myself included, recognizes those undesirable characteristics anymore.

We allow our horses to think and solve problems themselves. Then, we reward-reinforce the effort and thought process. Each time I teach them something particularly difficult, I keep in mind their different personalities. When we first worked with Mint, he clearly wasn't mentally involved in the training process. Now, he tries harder than any animal I have ever trained. George, on the other hand, eagerly tried to do whatever we asked. The problem was getting him to slow down and pay attention. He would try a hundred different things until he happened upon the correct answer. Standing still has been one of the hardest things for him to learn. With Mint, we reinforce for energy and enthusiasm, while George is reinforced for focus and deliberate behavior.

You can use the On Target Training system to shape any performance and attitude. If you want your horse to relax, reward-reinforce him when he exhales or when you feel him relax. If you want more energy, reward-reinforce him when he does something quickly or energetically. Figure out what characteristics you want to see more of in your horse's behavior. When we discuss **bridge-conditioning** later in the chapter, you'll learn how to draw attention to those characteristics so they become part of your horse's attitude. You will soon find yourself training "heart."

"OPERANT" CONDITIONING

The first behavioral concept I'll talk about is **operant conditioning.** We all learn through operant conditioning. Even a horse who has had no human contact learns through operant conditioning. This means the horse learns which behaviors get him what he wants and then he performs a particular behavior to achieve a specific result. In other words, he learns to "operate on his environment," hence the term operant (which comes from the Latin word for work) conditioning. Operant conditioning is primarily concerned with the relationship between animals and their environments. We define a horse's environment as everything and everyone around him. For example, why does a horse repeatedly contort his body into what appears to be an uncomfortable position to reach grass on the other side of the paddock fence? He does so because he reached greener or longer grass, a reinforcer, when he contorted himself to reach it the first time. The same is true for the foal who wanders over to another horse and is chased away. The youngster runs back to his dam for safety and learns that his mother's presence stops a frightening situation.

It is likely this young horse will repeat that behavior if he's scared again. He is operating on his environment to achieve a specific result.

I saw an amusing illustration of operant conditioning on a videotape. The tape showed a horse who operated on his environment by learning to kick an apple tree. He discovered this behavior quite by accident, I'm sure. Each time this horse kicked the tree, an apple fell for him to eat. He would kick the tree and turn to look for the fruit. It was clear the horse understood this instance of cause and effect. The horse got what he wanted by behaving in a certain way. The result of his action, an apple to eat, reinforced his behavior; therefore, the horse repeats that behavior when he wants the same result, another apple.

When training horses in our system, we work with the principles of operant conditioning. Understanding the importance of the environment in the learning process can help us to become more effective trainers. We are a significant part of our horses' environment. Therefore, our actions affect them. In our system, we concentrate primarily on what happens when a horse does something correctly. Since the outcome of a behavior determines whether the behavior will be repeated, we offer a reinforcement when a correct action is performed to increase the chances it will be repeated. The reinforcer, like the apple that falls from the tree, is one of the primary motivational ingredients in operant conditioning. Here is a textbook definition of a reinforcer out of Ferster and Culbertson's *Behavior Principles*. It's "the event which increases the frequency of the performance it follows." Read the definition a few times. Simply put, rewarded behavior is more likely to be repeated. Think of it in relation to the horse kicking the apple tree. The apple is the reinforcer. The horse repeats the action that caused the apple to fall from the tree. Using a reinforcer is a highly effective way to shape behavior.

PAVLOV'S DOGS

In the On Target Training system, we use a **bridge-signal** paired with an edible reinforcer to shape behavior. Pairing the bridge-signal, which is most often a clicker, with food is based on **classic behavioral conditioning.** Think of Pavlov and his dogs. The dogs were conditioned in the same way you will condition your horse to a bridge-signal. The sound of a bell was presented to the dogs just before every feeding. Soon, they associated the sound of the bell with food. The sound triggered a physical response.

The dogs salivated when they heard the bell because it had become associated with food. In the beginning of the experiment, the sound of the bell meant nothing to the dogs. Soon afterward, it meant they were going to eat. The bridge-signal will take on the same meaning to your horse. When I bridge-condition some horses, they actually salivate at the sound of the clicker, just as Pavlov's dogs did after associating the sound of the bell, their bridge-signal, with food (photo 11).

HERSHEY'S STORY

Next, I'd like to share with you a story that illustrates some of the material I've discussed about operant conditioning and shaping behavior. Hershey is our horse now, but when we first met him he operated on his environment in a way that intimidated the barn staff where he was stabled. You could say his actions actually shaped the behavior of his caretakers until I stepped in to rebalance the equation.

If you've ever been afraid to go into a horse's stall for fear of being kicked or bitten, you know just how dangerous and intimidating that can be. This was the situation I faced when I was asked to solve this highly successful "A"-circuit show-hunter's behavior problem.

As a youngster, this handsome brown gelding with a big, dark, kind eye had to endure a series of painful medical procedures. He was mistrustful of what people unfamiliar to him would do when they entered his stall. Perhaps this was the root of his actions. The bottom line, though, was that he was becoming more aggressive in his stall and the workers at the farm where he lived feared for their safety when feeding him. Who could blame them for being frightened? When they went into his stall, he would flatten his ears against his head and swing his hindquarters toward them, as if he was getting ready to kick.

On the other hand, when on the road traveling the show circuit, Hershey was cared for by a groom with whom he was comfortable. When she entered his stall, he would act a little grumpy, maybe pin his ears a bit, but he would not escalate stall hostilities any further. The trouble intensified between big shows, when he was on his home turf and under the care of a large staff. That's when his behavior needed intervention.

The first time I approached Hershey, I did so very carefully. I wasn't sure if he would actually kick or was just showing the warning signs that he was working up to it. I figured out pretty quickly that this horse was

I'm teaching George about bridge-conditioning. Note the clicker in my left hand while I feed him with the other.

quite smart and was actually training his handlers to feed him and get out of his stall as fast as they could! The more he threatened to act aggressively, the quicker the staff would do what they had to do and then get out of his way. As I walked up to his stall carrying his morning grain, he performed his usual feeding routine. He pinned his ears and turned his hind end toward me. I opened the door just a little, so I would be safe in case he decided to kick. He was not going to get the response he was expecting and there was a chance that he would feel frustrated and escalate the aggressive behavior. Instead, he flattened his ears against his head and waited. I waited, too. I didn't feed him and he stopped acting in a threatening way. He turned his head and looked at me with his ears pricked forward. Then he turned around to face me, relaxed and curious. He was trying to figure out why he wasn't getting food. It was actually very simple. The actions that got him fed quickly weren't working with me, and he wanted to eat.

When he turned his body to face me in a pleasant, non-aggressive manner, I gave him his food. From that day forward, the staff at the farm waited until Hershey behaved appropriately before they fed him. Without realizing it, the farm employees had been *reinforcing* Hershey's aggressive behavior by rewarding him with his meals when he acted in a threatening manner. Eventually, the staff didn't have to wait to feed him because he learned he was only reinforced for pleasant behavior. This was a case of understanding the various factors that shape behavior and using that information to change the way a horse responds.

AN INTRODUCTION TO THE BRIDGE-SIGNAL

A fundamental element of any successful training program is clear communication. A good line of communication hastens the training process. Without it, you set your horse and yourself up for frustration and disappointment. We use a bridge-signal to communicate with the horses in our training program. This signal is an integral component of our system. It relays to the horse a clear, consistent message. "Yes, what you are doing at this moment is correct. Return to me for a reward."

The bridge-signal got its name from its function. It actually bridges the gap between the moment the animal in training responds correctly, and the moment of reinforcement of that behavior. It also tells the animal that it has *completed* the behavior, and it can expect its reward. You will need to give another cue for the next behavior you want. Without the bridge-signal, reward-reinforcement can be ambiguous to the horse. In fact, offering a reward-reinforcement without the use of a bridge-signal can result in undesired behavior. When you offer reward-reinforcement without using the bridge-signal, the time gap between the performance of desired behavior and the opportunity to offer the reinforcement creates an opportunity for the horse to misinterpret which behavior is being rewarded.

Suppose you are teaching your horse to do canter departs without using a bridge-signal. He gives you the correct response. You stop your horse and reinforce him. He could very well associate the act of stopping with the reward, without making the connection to the correct canter depart. In this case, you may have just taught your horse to halt after each canter depart. I've seen a number of situations where horses would repeat the behavior immediately preceding reinforcement.

When implementing a bridge-signal in your training program, you eliminate some of the uncertainty for the horse. When a bridge-signal is used to identify the desired behavior prior to offering reward-reinforcement, you have clearly indicated the exact behavior you would like to see repeated. In the case of the canter depart, you would bridge to tell your horse that he's performing the action you desire the moment he responds correctly to your cue to canter. A bridge-signal helps to establish a clear and comprehensive system of communication by drawing your horse's attention to very specific behavior.

Earlier in the chapter, I discussed the meaning of a reinforcer. A reinforcer will increase the frequency of the behavior that occurred just before the reinforcer was offered. The bridge-signal itself has no meaning until it is paired with a **primary reinforcer** such as a carrot, a sugar cube, or a handful of grain. When the bridge-signal is paired with a primary reinforcer such as food, it takes on the same value as the food. Once that association is made, the bridge-signal itself becomes a reinforcer, just as the sound of the bell did for Pavlov's dogs. The same idea holds true for household cats who dash eagerly into the kitchen at the sound of a can opener. These cats have come to associate the sound of the can opener with getting food.

The bridge-signal can be just about anything you choose. It can be the sound of a whistle, a clicker, a snap of the fingers, a spoken word, or a touch. Whichever you choose, keep your bridge-signal distinct and quick to allow you to be precise with your communication.

If you've ever been to Sea World or another facility that trains marine mammals, you may remember hearing the sound of a high-pitched whistle at the whale or dolphin show. That sound was a bridge-signal. The sound of a whistle is distinct and it carries across the water. You also may have heard a word such as "okay" or the sound of a clicker in a show with walruses, sea lions, and otters. These types of bridge-signals work well because these animals tend to stay in closer proximity to the trainers than the larger marine mammals.

Horses also tend to stay in close proximity to their trainers. With horses, we prefer to use a clicker as a bridge-signal (photo 12). The sound of a clicker is easy for them to identify, and is a distinct sound they would not usually hear that draws their immediate attention. We discovered that the clicker works well at the beginning because horses are somewhat desensitized to the sound of human voices. They are accustomed to hearing us talking to them and people talking to each other. Later, when horses are further along in the On Target Training program, we usually switch to a distinct verbal bridge-signal. The advantage, once your horse fully understands the concept, is that you don't have to hold a clicker, freeing your hands for riding, longeing, clipping, and other activities.

However, when you start using the bridge-signal while riding, you should use the clicker to help your horse make the transition from groundwork to under-saddle work. Attach the clicker to a whip or riding crop to make signaling easier for you and clearer for him (photo 13).

Once your horse has mastered the concept of bridge-conditioning, it's time to teach him to do something worth bridging. If the only tool you had was a bridge-signal, you might wait all day to see the behavior you wanted to bridge. It helps to have tools to move the process along and guide your horse in the right direction. An excellent tool to accomplish this goal is the target, which we use as an extension of our hands (photo 14). With a target, you can physically guide a horse through behaviors, after you teach him to touch it. You can use a target to teach horses to lift their legs for hoof picking, lower their heads for clipping, and load easily into a trailer. Horses can be taught to hold on a target while being blanketed or when their stalls are picked out. You can teach them to lead or to stretch. The options are unlimited.

I will discuss details of the bridge-signal (bridge-conditioning) and the target (target-training) in Chapter Three.

HUSKER DU'S STORY

I'd next like to share another horse's story with you. The purpose of relating Husker Du's tale is twofold. This story offers a brief glimpse of the process of bridge-conditioning and **target-training.** (Refer to Chapter Three for more details.) It also reveals the strong association horses make with the On Target Training system, even in challenging circumstances when they haven't been reinforced for months, for instance. Here's the

12-13 You can use the clicker attached to your riding crop to make it easier to bridge-signal when you are riding.

story of the jumper that wouldn't come in from his paddock.

The first big snowfall of the winter in upstate New York left a blanket of white on the ground the day Husker Du refused to come in. He and several other horses at the stable had been turned out that morning. By midday, the grooms at the farm started bringing the horses back to the barn.

Everything was going smoothly until it was time to bring this particular horse inside. As a show jumper, he was used to regular handling and a daily routine and his behavior had not been troublesome on the ground or under saddle.

But, on that snowy day, this big, easygoing chestnut gelding acted in a most unusual way. When he saw one of his grooms walking toward his paddock, he veered away from the gate and galloped off to the other end. When efforts to coax him indoors became clearly futile and the groom turned away from him to leave, Husker Du charged back to the gate. When the groom so much as turned her head to look at him, he galloped away to the back of the paddock again. As the snow piled higher and the wind picked up, efforts were made by several of the grooms to lure him to shelter but all to no avail. Carrots and buckets of grain were offered as enticement, but as the day grew later and the weather more miserable, he simply would not be caught.

I'm still not sure why he behaved as he did. Something obvious only to him frightened him away from the people trying to catch him. After five hours of effort it looked to the discouraged grooms as though he'd be spending the night outdoors in the snow.

At the time, I was working with some of the other horses in training at this farm. As I got ready to leave, I sat in my car and watched the final unsuccessful attempts to catch this horse. I thought about some earlier work I had done with him and got an idea I hoped would work.

Several months before, this horse and I had become acquainted in Attitash, New Hampshire. He was one of a string of several horses being shown by a grand-prix rider while I was there solidifying my work using reward-reinforcement to train horses.

In the six days I worked with this horse, I visited his stall three times a day and spent approximately five minutes each session conditioning him to recognize the clicker as a bridge-signal. The first step I taught Husker Du was to understand what the bridge-signal meant. The next step was to teach him to touch a target with his nose; an act that earns the bridge-signal and the reward that follows (more on this in following chapters). This was the extent of my role in his training program. He was then ready for under-saddle work, so I turned him back over to his rider. This was my last encounter with the horse until that wintry day four months later.

Would he remember those summertime experiences and would I be able to apply them to the problem at hand? I was hopeful and got out of my car to give it a try. None of the grooms at the farm thought my idea would work, but at that point, nothing else had, and we all agreed it was worth a try.

I gathered my training tools: a bucket of grain, a clicker, and a target similar to the one I trained the horse to touch during the summer. As I expected, when I approached the paddock gate, he behaved the same way he had all day with his grooms. He stood there until he saw me and then spun and ran away. I watched with my peripheral vision and as I turned away from him, he galloped toward the gate again. I was hoping that my next action would strike a familiar chord with this jumper. Instead of trying to walk toward him to catch him as he approached the gate, I remained outside the paddock facing away from him and pressed the clicker as he came toward me. This time, he didn't flee. When I clicked, he stopped in his tracks and stood still with his ears pricked forward. Clearly, I had his complete attention. He seemed to remember what the distinct clicking sound meant, just as I'd hoped. The sound of the clicker told him that by moving toward the gate, he was behaving correctly and would get a reward when he came to me. Next, I took the target, turned toward him slowly, held it over the fence inside the paddock and said the word "target." As part of his earlier training, he had learned to touch the target with his nose in response to that word. He obviously remembered the experience. He walked up and touched the target just as he had been trained to do four months earlier at Attitash. I fed him some grain as his reward and he walked quietly with me to the paddock gate, then walked calmly with me all the way back to the barn. His earlier apprehension was gone.

The day Husker Du would not come in provided a huge learning experience for me. I learned that that his pleasant association with our training method was stronger than whatever had spooked him so consistently.

THE TRAINING GAME

When we do a clinic, I like to incorporate a little consciousness-raising. I want people who interact with horses to understand what it's like for animals to be trained—to become sensitized to the horse's point of view. For this purpose, we sometimes use "The Training Game," which was used to teach new trainers at Sea World. It's a powerful tool to demonstrate hands-on how it feels to learn through reward- versus removal-reinforcement.

Imagine being a stranger in a foreign land. No one speaks your language. You are powerless and unable to comprehend what is going on

14 Mint is happily touching his nose to the target and holding on it. I've taught him to follow it into the trailer (without halter or lead rope), focus on it to lower his head for clipping, and stand still for mounting.

around you. Your very survival could depend on behaving in a specific way that can't be explained to you because of differences in how you and these strangers communicate. Does this sound like the plot of the latest horror movie? This is the predicament, albeit somewhat overdramatized, that many horses experience during the training process.

How we communicate the behavior we desire from our horses can mean the difference between a willing horse, happy to do his job, or a surly, antagonistic horse, grudgingly working only when forced. This game also serves to demonstrate some of the fundamentals of On Target Training. Once you learn about The Training Game, you'll see how our techniques follow common sense and will be easy to keep using long after you finish this book.

Just about everyone who has participated in The Training Game has found it to be quite enlightening. Here's how it works. One or two people among the clinic group volunteer to be "trained." They leave the room. Then, the rest of the group decides what behavior they want to teach the volunteer, aka "the new horse," to do. It could be any simple behavior such as sitting on a chair, standing on one foot, or turning out the light.

When the volunteer returns to the group I take out a clicker to be used as a bridge-signal. I tell the volunteer that I will communicate only with this device, clicking to indicate when behavior is correct. The concept is like the guessing game we've all played as children, except that instead of using the word "warmer" to indicate good guesses, I communicate with the clicker to tell the "horse" she's getting closer to the right "answer."

In keeping with the concept of linking the sound of the clicker to something our human "horse" would like, I sometimes reinforce correct behavior with M & Ms or even money.

Let's suppose that the behavior we decide to train our new "horse" is to stand on a chair. I use the sound of the click and a treat—reward-reinforcement—as the horse takes steps toward accomplishing the desired behavior. I ignore undesired behavior.

Let's focus now on the question of how to train our "horse" to stand on a chair. The "horse" will probably come back into the room and wander about, trying to figure out what to do. At some point the "horse" will look toward the chair. I immediately click and reward to tell her she's on the right track. Movement toward the chair would be even better but it's unlikely that would happen right away. (Patience is part of The Training Game, just as it's part of your regular training program.) I continue to click and reward for each small step toward the behavior we are training. Each of these small steps is a building block to the larger, finished behavior. The "horse" has no way of knowing during the process what the end goal is, but with reward-reinforcement, the process itself is enjoyable.

Each time our "horse" takes another step toward the desired behavior, we are saying in a clear and pleasant way that she is doing the right thing. This is textbook behavioral conditioning and it works because each time our "horse" is reinforced this way, it increases the likelihood that she will repeat the behavior that was reinforced. And so the process continues until we get the desired behavior. In this case, our volunteer will ultimately stand on the chair and the rest of the group will cheer. The trainers are happy, the "horse" is happy, and the goal has been accomplished.

Once the volunteer has walked in the horse's hooves, her awareness, and the group's comprehension of the horse's learning process is enhanced.

When I first started conducting clinics to teach On Target Training, I used to use *removal-reinforcement* in The Training Game. Training through removal-reinforcement creates quite a different picture, and while maintaining the goal of getting the volunteer to stand on a chair, the training approach is quite different. If I was the "horse" and you were the trainer, you might push or prod me toward the chair I was to stand on. Under the removal-reinforcement system, you would stop pushing when I went toward the chair myself. What is reinforcing under these circumstances is the removal of the unpleasant sensation of prodding. So when you start pushing again, I have to figure out how to get you to stop. To avoid more poking, I must repeat the movement toward the chair.

When I was the "horse" during this removal-reinforcement training game, I found myself getting more and more annoyed by the process. I didn't like being poked (even though it didn't hurt) and prodded to be taught a behavior. In fact, I stopped doing it in my clinics because it created uncomfortable feelings of anger, apprehension, and frustration for the trainee and sometimes for the trainers too.

I've been the trainee or "horse" in both the reward- and removal-reinforcement training games, and I found it to be a significant learning tool to experience both approaches. My thoughts and feelings during each process were remarkably different. During the removal-reinforcement training game, I found myself putting a lot of effort into watching my "trainer's" hands to avoid being poked along. Although I was moving forward, I wasn't paying attention to figuring out what I was trying to accomplish. I was just trying to avoid the unpleasant sensation of being taught in this way. On the other hand, when reward-reinforcement was used, I concentrated on what I could do to be reinforced again. I remembered just what I was doing when I got reinforced and was eager to repeat the behavior.

Which way would you rather have your horse thinking during the training process? With reward-reinforcement, your horse will be eager to work for you and happy to build upon his training.

CHAPTER

Basic Training Principles

SETTING THE HORSE UP FOR SUCCESS

Setting a horse up to succeed is an invaluable training concept. Of course, you want your training to be successful, so think about how you can make this happen. Let's relate creating conditions for success to some elements of schooling we've already discussed. One of the ways we design the initial bridge-conditioning sessions for success is to reduce the size of the feed container you use for rewards. If you try this with your horse using a large bucket he can easily fit his head into, he will recognize and focus on the container only and be very persistent about trying to get to the food. Keeping his attention will be difficult, if not impossible. Instead, we recommend that you use a container I call a "side-bucket," small enough to cover with your hand or arm, so you can more readily control the food (photo 15). By not giving him the opportunity to be distracted by the grain, he will more likely concentrate on the choices you are offering and make the right decision.

When we initiate **target-training,** we stand right in front of the horse with the target, making it easy for him to touch it with his nose. Once he does, and we establish a few "bridges," he begins to understand what we're asking and can make the right decision. Once again, this sets the horse up

15 An appropriately-sized container to use as your "side-bucket" for food. It should be attached to your waist so you have both hands free. (A hiker's waist-pack is a good alternative, particularly if it is lined.)

for success. Then we begin to move the target away from him, a little bit at a time. The horse's thought process becomes evident as he makes deliberate movements toward the target.

Typically, we initiate target-training in a stall or pasture, somewhere that is familiar and comfortable for the horse to allow him to focus on us. If we were to start the process at a show or somewhere less familiar to the horse, we would need to spend more time and be more patient since his attention would obviously be more easily diverted.

Let's say you want to teach a young horse to stand quietly in the aisle for grooming. Do you think it would be better to start the lesson in the morning while other horses are still being fed, or later in the afternoon after the horse has been turned out for a few hours? Clearly, he is more likely to be relaxed following a few hours of turnout. Choosing a time when the horse is relaxed will give you more of his attention and allow more opportunities for reinforcement, setting him up for success. Remember, the more reinforcement the horse gets for an action, the more likely he will be to repeat the desired behavior.

So, although you may not always want to groom your horse after turnout, this time frame will give you the best chance to communicate the desired behavior and set him up for success at the beginning. Once he understands the **criteria**—what you are asking him to do—you can switch times. Be aware that when you do switch the time or place, performance may initially decrease. This is absolutely normal! Do what you can to get your horse back on the right track. If necessary, take a step back in training so you can bridge-condition to communicate what you are teaching. Be patient. Wait for the horse to make the correct decision.

Let me give you an example. You may start target-training in his stall. You work with him until he clearly understands the concept. He is "targeting" perfectly. Next, you decide to work with target-training in the ring. At first, your horse may not even look at the target. So you must lower your expectations. Before you move from the stall to the ring, realize that your horse may be distracted. Your initial step should be to get him to focus and touch the target. Make it easy for him to succeed by putting the target directly in front of him (photo 16). Since the session is more difficult in a new environment, keep it short. Your actual goal in this circumstance is to get your horse to focus on you. So begin a few steps back from where the last session ended to enable him to succeed. In the next couple of sessions, you can gradually raise the level of difficulty. The initial process takes some time and patience, but in the long run, progress will be much quicker when you take all the time you need to lay the proper foundation. Remember, slow down. You'll go faster.

Bridge-conditioning and target-training teach the horse to focus on you and to pay attention to your requests. The bridge-conditioning and the target are simply tools to teach and communicate the value of listening. It is important to teach your horse to pay attention and respect you. This can be achieved rather quickly during the On Target Training process.

16   When you first introduce the target, make sure your horse can easily (even accidentally) touch it, so you can bridge and reinforce him immediately.

(Chapter Three will provide detailed instructions.) Teach your horse to make eye contact with you while he's standing quietly, preferably in his stall. Start teaching eye contact when you bridge-condition, which is when he first learns to focus on you. Your horse will learn quickly that he must pay attention to your cues to get reinforcement. A large percentage of his distractions will be eliminated when he learns to focus solely on you whether you are standing by his side or riding him. By noticing your horse's focus, and bridge-conditioning when he is attentive, you will train him to concentrate on you more and more.

HOW HORSES THINK

Behavioral experts have debated for decades how to define and measure intelligence. I don't have all the answers to those big questions, but I have spent quite a bit of time observing the attitude and aptitude of several animal species, including, of course, horses. I am often asked how I would compare the intelligence of horses to killer whales. When Vinton and I were in the early stages of developing the On Target Training system, some experienced horsemen raised an interesting objection; they thought horses weren't smart enough for this training method. But, people have been astounded by our teaching horses to touch their noses to a target, and how we teach horses in less than a minute to turn their heads away from us. Like marine mammals, horses are naturally curious. On Target Training increases a horse's focus and natural inclination to solve the "puzzle." This makes them excellent students!

I have successfully used the same approach with horses and killer whales as well as with dolphins, walruses, otters, dogs, sea lions, donkeys, mustangs, and a zebra. For nearly all the species I've worked with, the initial stages of teaching occur similarly. The otters were the exception. They routinely needed more repetition than the others to learn a behavior. Learning tendencies differ most among the species I've worked with when teaching complex actions. Killer whales and dolphins seem to have an aptitude for complex thought and are able to connect more than one idea and quickly understand new concepts. With that quick intelligence comes a desire to play games and test their trainers! Killer whales are the top predators in the ocean, which enables them to remain confident, focused, and pretty unflappable. In fact, after the baby killer whale was born at Sea World, we noticed she never seemed to have much reaction to sudden noises or movement. Nothing seemed to scare her. I found her demeanor quite intriguing so I decided to experiment. I didn't want to frighten her, but I wanted to learn more about her extraordinary confidence. In an effort to startle her, I started with small surprises and built up to actions that would startle most humans like jumping out from behind pillars or walls. Instead of a startled reaction, she seemed to find it all delightful fun and seemed to get more curious about what I might do next! Her behavior epitomized what you might expect from a top predator.

Interestingly, I have found horses and sea lions similar to train. Both species are lower in the food chain and seem to always have an eye out for predators, making them somewhat skittish, particularly in new places. We even teach them some similar behaviors. At Sea World, sea lions are taught to ride on golf carts through the park. Teaching a sea lion to ride on a moving vehicle is remarkably like teaching a horse to ride in a trailer. The sea lions in the Sea Lion and Otter Show appear as though riding on the back of a cart is completely natural for them. In reality, training them to do this can be an arduous process. First, you must build up their confidence being on the cart itself. Then, they have to learn to get comfortable with its movement and trusting enough to travel to unfamiliar places in the park. When they get nervous, they tend to flee to the nearest body of water, whether that pool contains dolphins, sea turtles, or sharks. No restraining devices are used on the sea lions so they must be solid at riding on the cart before trainers can risk traveling to different areas of the park.

Horses are also flight animals and, by nature, respond quickly to new situations. This makes them fast learners, which is one of the reasons immediate reinforcement is important. To safeguard their survival, horses deduce quickly. When you give a bridge-signal for performing a behavior, your horse will remember what action got him the signal for food and is likely to repeat it. When we train in this manner, we are teaching our horses to think. We are allowing them to make a choice to get their reward.

At first, these decisions should be small ones. For instance, the horse should not "choose" to put his head in the side-bucket where we carry the feed while we are bridge-conditioning him (photo 17). We wait out the incorrect option until he chooses the correct behavior, in this instance, not putting his head in the side-bucket. We only feed the horse when he makes the correct choice. The same process occurs when we target-train. He gets bridged and reinforced with food when he responds correctly, which in this case would be touching the target at the end of the stick.

17   I'm ignoring and "waiting-out" George's incorrect behavior. He is trying to help himself to the food in my side-bucket, and I've covered it so
he cannot get any. When he realizes he has got to move his head away—making the
correct choice in this situation—I'll bridge-reinforce him.

The horse may walk around in his stall. He may touch the wrong end of the stick—the handle end, and not the target itself. These are all choices, although not the correct ones. Still, they are indicative of progress. It is normal to see incorrect decisions, particularly in the beginning of the training process. Often, the horse is testing to see what will happen. We wait him out, ignore the wrong choices, and draw attention to correct decisions, even small ones, by bridging them. Once your horse knows what is expected, you will see more and more correct decisions. In traditional training programs, horses are usually not stimulated to think and make choices. As soon as they do something wrong, they are corrected and, in the process, are taught to react. By adding On Target Training to your program, you are factoring in a way to encourage your horse to think about how he can obtain a reward.

An advantage to working with horses over marine mammals is that horses are grazers, designed to eat frequently. Marine mammals become satiated at certain times. They have periods of eating when they gorge themselves and periods of fasting when they won't eat. We try to balance this out by regulating their food intake through smaller, more frequent meals. Horses always seem to want to eat, which makes training through reward-reinforcement even easier than it is with marine mammals.

Horses are social animals and learn by imitating others in the herd. You can discover a lot about your horse by watching him interact with other horses, even from afar. You can also glean information about him and how he deals with his environment by observing his body language and tendencies. A word of caution here: observing equine behavior is useful; imitating equine behavior as a means of communication can be dangerous and inappropriate. I don't recommend such a practice. Horses regularly establish and change the herd pecking order by challenging each other. They displace and intimidate each other by rearing, striking, and kicking. Horses communicate with each other in this very physical manner, but humans should only use their intellect to take the higher and more effective road by building a relationship based on trust and respect.

MAKING HISTORY: REINFORCEMENT-HISTORY, THAT IS!

Now, let's focus on understanding why horses behave as they do. Understanding why horses act in certain ways makes it easier to change or modify their behavior. Essentially, a horse behaves the way he does because he has been reinforced by changes in his environment that have resulted from his actions. A pattern becomes established that is known as **reinforcement-history.**

For instance, a horse who repeatedly raises his head to avoid having his ears touched has figured out that this action works. Each time he lifts his head and keeps his ears from being touched increases the likelihood he will do it again because he got reinforced the last time. By avoiding the aversive (your hand) with this behavior, he establishes and builds a reinforcement-history.

Just about every human or animal behavior results from a reinforcement-history. When we walk into a dark room, even if it's an unfamiliar room, we reach for the wall near the door looking for a light switch. When we flip the light switch, we are reinforced by gaining our objective, light in the room. We reach for the switch by the door on the wall because that's usually where we've found it previously. We have a reinforcement-history with this action and we repeat it regularly.

Naturally, the action of flipping a light switch isn't always successful. Sometimes you'll go somewhere where the light switch doesn't work. To get light, you have to enter the room and manually turn on a lamp. When you're back in that room or house, do you stop trying to flip on the wall switch? Not for quite a while. Flipping on a wall switch has become a habit, but in time, this behavior would change if you had to turn on a lamp switch instead. Modification comes about in this case because of a revised reinforcement-history. If wall switches all over the world stopped working, flipping the switch would soon be gone from our repertoires.

Everything your horse does or doesn't do is because of a reinforcement-history, too. Whenever your horse is doing something, there is a reason for his actions. Your horse has learned to act or react the way he does because of a history of trying to get something he desires, or avoiding something he doesn't like.

Now, let's get back to the horse who has a habit of not letting you touch his ears. Many horses are sensitive about their ears and a common response seems to be to lift their heads to avoid being touched. Here's how a reinforcement-history like this could have developed. At first, when you tried to touch this horse's ears, he might have become a little tense and raised his head. You tried again and he responded the same way. This response, as we've seen, is reinforcing his action by avoiding the aversive stimulus of the hand touching the ears. Next, he begins to put the pieces together. The hand goes up toward his head, his head moves up higher than the hand, and this equals no contact with the ears! It becomes a routine or habit. Soon, he doesn't even think about it. He just does it. This repeated behavior is in sync with his reinforcement-history.

Suppose you decide that enough is enough. It's time to change this behavior. You want your horse to be amenable to having his ears touched but to change his pattern requires motivation. What is the best motivator available? The answer is food, a primary reinforcement.

If your horse has been avoiding having his ears touched for years, it will take longer to "rebalance the scales" than if this is a recent development in his behavior. The rebalancing may also take longer if your horse experienced some trauma related to having his ears touched. In that circumstance, you may need to spend more time rebuilding his history. However, no matter what his history has been you can change his present behavior and teach your horse to lower his head and offer you his ears. Once you have established the correct reinforcement-history, he will want, even be eager, to do what you ask of him.

With consistent effort, you can change your horse's reinforcement-history. Start the process by working in small increments, with lots of reinforcement for each little step toward the desired behavior. (For specific detail, see the section on clipping in Chapter Four.) With each small step you add more weight to the side of the scale that represents the reinforcement-history you want to establish.

TRAINING CREDOS

At Sea World, we taught animals to do amazing things. You may have seen the spectacular performances in the shows. In addition to those examples of dramatic training, we taught them husbandry behavior such as remaining still to allow blood samples to be drawn, traveling in transport vehicles, or volunteering urine or milk samples. One whale who required dental work learned to keep his mouth open while his teeth were drilled and cleaned.

Captive whales and dolphins work and play in a controlled environment. They are taught behaviors in that familiar, predictable atmosphere. Once the animals know their behaviors and are performing them regularly, there is little additional input required from the trainers. The trainers provide cues to communicate when and how long to perform specific behaviors. The stable environment reduces the variables.

Working with horses is different. There is an amazing amount of team work involved, along with a great many variables to deal with on a regular basis. With horses, there are constant changes in the environment. You need your horse to be responsive and compliant, especially as you begin to do more things with him. Naturally, you want to eliminate balking and spooking as much as possible, since these behaviors could result in injury. That's why it's important to develop focus as well as trust between horse and rider and to foster a partnership.

When I was first learning to ride, what impressed me the most is the partnership between horse and rider. A partnership goes both ways. You need to be able to trust your horse. To develop a rider's trust, a horse needs to consistently listen and respond. Likewise, your horse needs to trust you to be consistent and reliable. This type of relationship is not built on fear. On the contrary, a truly responsive and compliant horse is relaxed and alert, impossible to achieve in a relationship based on fear. Fright results in anxiety and tension, conditions that do not bring out the best qualities in either a human or equine partner. That's why nervousness has no place in the partnership equation. In any environment or situation, make a strong effort to minimize your horse's nervousness.

No matter what your training plans are for your horse, you want a horse who listens and is responsive. The most effective way to achieve this is to build up an appropriate reinforcement-history, using reward-reinforcement or removal-reinforcement. As we discussed earlier, both methods when used properly are very effective training tools. However, since removal-reinforcement tends to achieve results with the unwelcome possibility of greater frustration and less motivation from the horse, we focus on reward-reinforcement. Even complicated behaviors that involve great effort can be attained solely through reward-reinforcement.

Incorporating reward-reinforcement into your training program can change your horse's attitude about your partnership. With this approach, horses actually begin to look forward to working with you. In the beginning of the training process, they connect these actions with getting fed. We have all witnessed the great lengths horses will go to for food. Soon, the association with food becomes linked to the whole training experience, and your presence becomes a conditioned reinforcer. Your horse will be eager to be with you since he'll connect you with the schooling sessions during which he is fed. There have been times when someone mistakenly fed our horses their dinner when we were planning to do a training session. Even though they had food in front of them, they voluntarily left that meal to come out and work. Once, when I took our horses out for a training session, I discovered they were not hungry. They weren't sick but probably had little appetite since they had spent eight hours traveling on the trailer, which was a new experience for them. Also, it was one of the first hot, humid spring days. Neither horse ate, yet they performed every behavior perfectly. These situations clearly show that their association with Vinton and me involves much more than just the food or their appetite. Our horses definitely want to please us. That is what I want from a partner.

Every interaction with horses is a time of learning. One of the lessons your horse is constantly learning is what he can get away with and what you won't allow. You are always working on your relationship and trust when you are with your horse. Remember, your behavior influences your partner's behavior.

A key concept in training is to be aware of your horse's good behavior. Don't ignore what he normally does well. When your horse stands quietly for clipping, or loads calmly into the trailer, let him know from time to time that this behavior is worth recognizing. Remember: never take good behavior for granted.

This point brings up another very important basic training rule: draw attention to desired behavior and ignore unwanted behavior. Vinton and I once met a boarder at a barn where we worked who was eager to discuss a problem she was having with her horse. She had taught her mare to "shake hands" while cross-tied in the aisle. The woman would reach out her hand and the horse would raise her front foot. She reinforced this behavior with a carrot or other treat. This mare's action turned into a problem when she repeatedly lifted her feet even without being asked. Her pawing was something we refer to as "soliciting." She was trying to get more carrots.

Vinton and I learned that the only time this mare received carrots on a consistent basis was when her owner asked her to "shake hands." We realized that this horse was trying to get more treats by performing the only behavior for which she received food. To solve this problem, we needed to rebalance the mare's reinforcement-history. We explained the On Target Training system to the owner and had her introduce the bridge-signal so she could communicate more effectively with her mare. When the mare understood what the bridge-signal meant, the owner bridged and fed her while she was standing still in the cross-ties. We showed this owner how to realign her mare's reinforcement-history by making it more worthwhile for her to stand quietly than for her to "shake hands." During the process, she ignored the pawing when it occurred. Instead, she drew attention to the behavior we desired, standing quietly. The horse soon stopped the annoying, unintentionally-trained behavior and only offered her hoof to "shake hands" when given the cue.

SUPERSTITIOUS BEHAVIOR

Another issue to be aware of is superstitious behavior. This is behavior that is accidentally reinforced; an unintentional action that the animal comes to believe is part of the expected standard. For example, Mint believed he had to walk around his stall in a clockwise direction to go to his stationary target in the corner directly behind him. He had learned this because in his previous stall, his target had been in the other corner, diagonally opposite to his stall door. So now when given the cue, he was taking a longer route than necessary to the target. Once I recognized that this was happening, I went into his stall and pointed him directly to his target, and then reinforced him (photo 18).

Another example of superstitious behavior involved a dolphin. This dolphin was learning to do a back-flip. He was a show dolphin who lived in the dolphin lagoon, a natural, murky section you couldn't see through. This dolphin was given the cue to do a back-flip. As part of the performance, he was to follow a target that was tapped on the surface of the water in the center of the lagoon. (When teaching aerial behavior like this, the animals are guided through the behavior with a target, in this case one on a long pole.) It took him longer to reach the target than it should have, but once he got there, he followed the target well and did a great early learning attempt at a back-flip. He was bridged and fed for his extraordinary effort. Again, he was sent to perform a back-flip, and again he took a long time to reach the target but made great performance progress once he got to the target. It was decided not to make an issue of the length of time it took for him to get to the target since his back-flips were coming along so well. Pretty soon, he started doing shows. The trainers worked out the awkward timing problem by sending him out first and then waiting a few seconds before starting the other dolphins. They all arrived together for a back-flip. Sometime later, this dolphin was moved to a pool

18 I've sent George to hold on his stationary target in his stall, and I'll wait for a minute before I bridge-reinforce him. Note his ears are back, listening for the bridge-signal.

where you could see through the water and was asked to do a back-flip. It became clear what took this dolphin longer than the others. He had a whole underwater routine he did in exactly the same way each time he was sent to do a back-flip that he thought was a required action.

Generally it's easy to eliminate superstitious behavior, once you recognize it. When Vinton and I first trained our horses to spin, I gave the cue and Vinton guided them through the behavior with a target. One day, Vinton was doing the training sessions with the horses and gave the cue for a spin. He thought he gave them the same cue I did, but each horse just looked at him. We analyzed what I did when I asked for the spin and discovered that I took a step in the direction I wanted the spin to go. This was the key. A superstitious behavior that I was doing had become part of my cue. We corrected the problem by reintroducing the target during Vinton's sessions. The horses understood what was requested right away. In my sessions, I just faded my step out of the cue. It was an easy problem to solve. Being aware of the potential for superstitious behavior will help you prevent it from becoming part of your horse's repertoire.

USING A THREE-SECOND PAUSE

In the training process, things won't always go as you plan. Your timing may be off and you might inadvertently miss reinforcing the behavior you are training. You may accidentally bridge incorrect behavior. Or your horse may do the wrong thing or make an incorrect decision. If that happens, the best thing to do is pause for three seconds. Simply stand quietly and behave in a neutral manner (photo 19). After three seconds, continue with the training session. A pause each time something goes wrong in the session communicates to the horse that he's not going to be reinforced because he did not perform the correct behavior.

At Sea World, we used a three-second pause in response to undesirable behavior. We found this to be the least reinforcing stimulus we could offer. The results of the three-second pause proved highly successful.

There was a time at Sea World when we didn't uniformly apply the three-second pause. Each trainer responded differently to unwanted actions. They showed their displeasure in a variety of ways, some mild, some a bit more dramatic, such as kicking over buckets or stomping feet. During this time, the whales' incorrect responses actually started to increase. They seemed to enjoy the trainers' antics and found the reac-

19   George is doing a back-up, but quits before I tell him with the bridge-signal. I communicate to him that he made an incorrect decision by "pausing"—I stand still and don't do anything—for three seconds. Most horses figure out the meaning of the "pause" early in their training.

tions reinforcing, although clearly the trainers did not intend for this to be the case. To minimize the variance of responses, we developed the three-second pause. We found that remaining still for three seconds didn't inadvertently reinforce the whales. They learned that this pause meant they were not going to get reinforced, which communicated clearly that they had performed an undesirable behavior.

Consistency is one of the most important aspects of all training, especially with incorrect behavior. If you consistently use a three-second pause after an undesired action, you will see that action decrease. Conversely, by drawing attention to desired behavior through reward- or removal-reinforcement, you will see an increase in the behavior you want.

Another point to remember is that horses are intended by nature to live in herds. They respond to the activities of those around them. How many times have you seen one horse startle just because another horse, or even a person, jumps? They rely on members of the herd to alert each other to danger. They constantly react to the behavior of others to survive. Since we are part of their environment, humans exert a strong influence on horses. Accordingly, try to minimize your reactions. If you become tense, so will your horse. If your horse spooks in the cross-ties, try not to respond angrily or abruptly. Instead, be relaxed and confident. The nervous horse that doesn't want to go in the trailer will usually become more rattled if you react in an anxious or angry manner. I have seen on more than one occasion an upset, reluctant loader walk into the trailer just when everyone who was trying to get him on stopped tugging and pulling. So remember not to become excited or emotional in response to undesired behavior. It doesn't help your horse to relax, concentrate, or make correct decisions.

FADING-OUT THE TRAINING TOOLS

When you teach your horse something new, you may need to use certain tools to help him understand the concept. These tools and techniques help set your horse up to succeed by guiding him toward steps in the process worth bridging. As you progress toward your training goal, you'll want to streamline the intermediate steps and fade-out the tools. Here are two examples of fading-out tools from the lesson.

I worked with Theo who reared, spun, and behaved in a dangerous manner when a professional rider attempted to mount. Before addressing the mounting issue, I worked with Theo in his stall, going through the steps of bridge-conditioning and target-training. Once I was sure he clearly understood the meaning of these tools, I took steps toward resolving his mounting problem. After Theo was tacked up, I led him to the mounting block and asked him to touch his nose to the hand-held target. I bridged and reinforced his correct response. Next, while he was at the mounting block, I held the rein close to the bit and asked him to touch the target. When he calmly touched it, I bridged and reinforced his correct action. As the next step, I introduced the rider to the scenario. As she placed her foot in the stirrup and shifted her weight to get on, I held the rein and asked him to touch the target, just as I did in the previous step. Theo did exactly what I asked of him. He calmly touched the target and didn't even flinch when he felt the rider ease into the saddle. He was more focused on the target and getting a reward than he was with the rider's presence. I fed him a few handfuls of feed and concluded the lesson. The next day, I went through the same procedure but faded-out one of the tools. I didn't hold the rein. Since that step went well, I faded-out the target in our next session. The next day, I held the target by my side but didn't ask Theo to touch it. He stood quietly as the rider got on and I had her feed him, which led to the next step, fading me out of the picture so Theo would concentrate on his rider. I did that the next day by standing several feet away as the rider mounted and reinforced his quiet, calm demeanor. After that point, Theo was fine about standing quietly as a rider got in the saddle.

There are many different ways to solve this particular problem and, of course, to fade-out the training tools. (See Chapter Five for more details on mounting.) If the horse has difficulty with a step, keep the training tool in place until he understands the task. If we went back to the previous example with Theo, and if he had been a bit slower about learning the lesson of standing quietly and fidgeted, I would still reinforce him since fidgeting is still better than rearing and bolting, but I would not fade-out the target until he stood completely still. Going too slow is better than going too fast. Remember: slow down, you'll go faster.

The next example involves our horse Hershey. We were teaching him to back up from the ground, which involved me standing facing him. I gave him the cue and Vinton put the target just below Hershey's nose and moved it back toward his chest. As he tried to touch his nose to the target, he had to step back in order to follow the movement. For the finished product, he would back up between ten and thirty steps with just the cue, stopping when he heard the bridge. We have had much success using this technique to teach horses to back up. When we train this routine, we break it up into small approximations, starting with following the target back one step at a time until he walks back ten to fifteen steps. Then, we begin to fade-out the target. We start by dropping it to our side, but still walk back with the horse and bridge and reinforce even the smallest commitment to walking back without the target. At this point, you can really see the horses think, which we bridge and reinforce. Once they consistently take a step or two without the target, we keep up the momentum by holding the target out on the third step. We proceed like this until the horse confidently backs without the target. The next step is fading-out the second person by having him stand further back or off to the side. We decide how to fade-out the second person based on the horse's progress. (It's always good to be flexible and pay attention to the horse.) Next, I watch for the horse's attention to shift from the second person to his task of backing. As soon as I see the horse focus on what he's doing, I bridge and reinforce.

In Hershey's case, we had a difficult time. We had already worked with him enough to know he's a quick learner, but this pattern proved to be a challenge to his thought process. He did fine with the target but the trouble began when we attempted to fade it out of the process. Hershey kept turning to face and follow Vinton. He clearly didn't understand the concept we were teaching. We solved this by putting the target in and out as they walked back. I tried to bridge and reinforce mostly when the target wasn't present and when he was backing straight. Next, we tried to fade-out Vinton's position. However, he wouldn't back without Vinton walking with him. We tried putting Vinton further back so Hershey would have to start to back up to reach Vinton, but Hershey tried to face Vinton. We tried moving Vinton to the side but Hershey would adjust his movement to get closer to Vinton. I could get him to back one or two steps if I gave him the cue and stepped toward him but he wouldn't follow through. We reintroduced the target, using the same concept I used with the otters, a lot of repetition. We worked with him over the course of a few weeks, using the target to have him back ten to fifteen steps. Sometimes I bridged and reinforced the movement of his hind legs, sometimes the movement of his front legs. I also bridged and reinforced when he concentrated on his actions, not the target. After the extra few weeks, the fading-out process worked quite well. Now, Hershey backs like our other horses.

The steps you use to train your horse as well as the steps you use to fade-out the various training tools will vary from horse to horse. There is no set formula. These two anecdotes should give you some guidelines on how to fade-out the tools, but you need to adapt them to your horse and situation. Don't hesitate to be creative.

CHAPTER

Start Training!

B To start the bridge-conditioning process, you will need your bridge-signal and a side-bucket, waist pack, or easily accessed pocket to contain food. It's best to have the food right with you but to keep your hands free. I refer to the sound of the clicker as the bridge-signal in the following narrative because that's what we use in our program. I prefer to start the process in a controlled environment like a horse's stall or another place where he is most comfortable and least able to be distracted. If your horse lives outside, you can start him there, although it will be difficult if other horses are interested in the feed. After you begin the process, you can do training sessions just about anywhere. Indeed, there are advantages to varying the training locales, as you'll see.

When you first enter the stall, your horse will not understand your purpose in being there. He'll know you have food with you and he'll naturally be very interested in eating, so it's best if you can cover the food with your hand or arm to prevent him from helping himself. As I begin the conditioning process, I set only one criterion. I don't want the horse to be pushy about getting food. If your horse behaves in this manner, and he most likely will, be patient. After all, he's probably used to having food brought in and put into his feed tub and doesn't yet know the new rules. He's just trying to eat the food as he's always done. He will eventually give up and look away. If he gets too aggressive, you may have to shoo him away. However, the moment he looks away, press the clicker, and immediately feed him out of your hand. The only time you should not bridge is when your horse has his nose in the food source, or on your hands or body. He can be looking away or making eye contact with you. It doesn't matter. At this point, all you're doing is pairing the sound of the clicker with the presentation of food, a primary reinforcer.

When you enter their stalls with food, many horses become assertive about obtaining the meal. By trying to put their noses in the food bucket and eat, they are attempting to get what they want from their environment. This can be uncomfortable and even intimidating to the person with the feed. Later in this chapter, I'll tell the story of a domineering German warmblood who led us to derive the technique described above. We teach horses that pushiness is not an effective tool to get the food, but turning their heads away from the person with the food works well. Again, the technique is to bridge and reinforce the horse as soon as he looks away, whether he does this because he gave up being pushy, was distracted by something in his environment, or because he was shooed away. If he keeps his head turned away while he's chewing, bridge and reinforce him again (photos 20 and 21). Continue with this process, and usually within a minute, the horse learns that pushy behavior gets him nothing. He will begin turning his head away with the same degree of enthusiasm he had been putting into mugging you for the food. In this instance, the horse is learning a different way of operating on his environment by repeating the behavior that previously worked to get him what he wants. This lesson teaches the horse to respect your space. We have also utilized this technique to cure "mouthy" horses and biters. Most likely, you will see your horse keep his eye on you while he turns his head away. You'll also observe his pushiness subside.

Once the horse is more respectful of your space and is not demanding the food, make eye contact the criterion for bridging and reinforcing him. This will result in a more attentive horse who focuses on you without crowding you.

The food should always be presented immediately after the sound of the clicker to make sure the horse comes to associate this sound with the food. The process is click, feed; click, feed, until the container of food is consumed. When you feed, hold your hand out a bit instead of feeding close to the container. This helps to reduce his focus on the location of the food. Next, walk around the stall. When your horse follows, bridge and

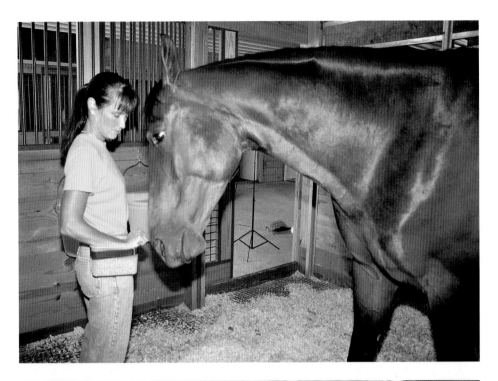

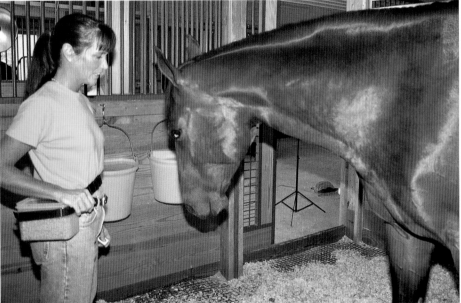

20-21   First, George is focusing only on the food in my side-bucket that I'm covering with my hand. As soon as he turns away, I tell him he's made the correct choice by clicking and then reinforcing this signal with some food. This is called bridge-conditioning.

feed. He will quickly learn to stay with you. After two or three training sessions, you can wait a second or two between clicks, but be sure to always feed immediately after bridging. The brief pause between clicks helps build up some anticipation and keeps the horse attentive. Remember the criterion of no pushiness. Gradually increase the time between clicks. This will increase your horse's level of patience.

Ideally, I like to bridge-condition three times a day and spend five to ten minutes on each session for approximately three to four days. However, not everyone can spend that amount of time at the barn or stables. Even if you only have time to see your horse a few times a week, you can still condition him to the bridge-signal. Naturally, the more often you do the conditioning work, the more quickly he will comprehend it. Do sessions every twenty minutes if that works in your schedule. Or spend five minutes on a session when you first get to the barn and five minutes on a session before you leave. After four days, your horse should be quite solid with the bridge-signal. No matter what your time frame for accomplishing bridge-conditioning, your horse will retain what he has learned. Do you recall the story I told earlier about Husker Du who wouldn't be caught in his paddock? He remembered the bridge-conditioning I had done with him months before.

After you've done several bridge-conditioning sessions, you may see your horse's ears prick forward when you give him the bridge-signal. It will be obvious he recognizes the signal and is anticipating the presentation of food.

I found one horse I worked with especially intimidating while I bridge-conditioned him. When I entered his stall for the first time, this massive German-bred horse acted in a domineering way. Even though he had recently been gelded, he was still displaying stallion-like aggressive behavior and was less than pleased that I had food but was not putting it in the feed tub for him. He loomed over me with his head and neck. When I found myself pinned against the wall, I knew I needed to teach him to give me more space. It took about forty-five seconds before he looked away from me toward the people standing outside his stall. I bridged this behavior and fed him. I wanted to maintain some distance between us. He was so close to me I couldn't establish eye contact. I waited until he looked out of his stall again before I bridged and fed him. Within a minute of the first bridge, he solved the puzzle. He figured out what he had to do to get fed. He then turned his head toward the barn aisle but his eyes never left me. His behavior was very deliberate. He was no longer looking outside the stall, but turning his head and neck while still focusing on me.

This was one of the first horses I worked with and this experience illustrated how quickly horses can learn, which makes sense when you think about their place in the food chain. Horses are prey animals whose survival depends on quick thinking. I've learned through the many horses I worked with that they are good problem solvers and quick learners when given the opportunity.

Bridge-conditioning a green horse who has not had much human contact will most likely take a little bit more patience than bridge-conditioning a more experienced horse. To begin, I would initiate bridge-conditioning at feeding time, using the food rationed for the meal. If you normally feed half-a-quart of pellets for the evening meal, use that food at the usual time. He will be anticipating his meal, feeling hungry, and likely to be bolder since he'll be eager to eat. Taking advantage of this interest will help set him up to succeed.

It's best to begin bridge-conditioning the horse alone so that he can focus better on you. If there are other horses where he can see them, that's fine. However, if they are in the same field or paddock, you'll find yourself fending them off. Also, if your horse is not dominant in the social order, he will probably be pushed away by the other horses. It's possible but difficult to work with a group, so separate the horse you want from the rest of the herd.

If your horse is not accustomed to people, it may take a while to build up enough trust for him just to eat from your hand. You may even need to start by allowing him to eat from a scoop and then progress to eating from your hand. Let's say you're in a stall with a reluctant weanling. The best way to start is to consider the horse's nature. What can you do to be less intimidating to him? You can crouch down, making yourself seem smaller and less threatening. Staying crouched in one place — the corner — will encourage him to approach you. This will help him become bolder. It also works to crouch low if you are out in a field and trying to get your skittish horse to approach you (photo 22). You can turn and walk away a short distance, then squat low and wait with some food. When he learns that you have the food, and are safe to approach, he will improve by leaps and bounds. Then you can proceed with bridge-conditioning.

It is important to keep in mind the power of the bridge-signal as a reinforcer. It increases the likelihood that any single action or behavior that

22 I'm crouching here with Dandy, a five-month-old Quarter Horse. This was his first day at our farm, and he was understandably apprehensive. I'm trying to make myself appear small, thus less threatening to him.

precedes your giving the signal is likely to be repeated. So if you accidentally bridge your horse at the wrong time, you must respond immediately by pausing for a few seconds and not follow this mistimed bridge with a reward. For example, if you are trying to teach your horse to hold his leg up but you miss the timing and bridge him just as he is putting it back down, do not feed him but just pause for three seconds. Then cue him to lift his leg again and try to bridge him at the right moment while he is still holding it up. Sometimes you may have to go back a step in training to get on the right track again, but the system is quite forgiving, and an occasional mishap like this does not hamper progress for long.

Even more importantly, be careful to never misuse the bridge-signal. A riding teacher told me a story involving one of her school horses. She used the clicker when the horse started to run away with one of her students to get him to come back. The horse returned but, as you can guess, at the first opportunity ran away again! By bridging him at that moment the teacher had simply rewarded him for running away, a dangerous action nobody wanted him to repeat.

Once your horse understands that the bridge-signal means that he will be reinforced, it's time to move on to the next step. From this point on in On Target Training, the clicker will have reinforcing value for your horse. Your horse will soon focus more on the bridge-signal than on the food. Now you'll be able to use the bridge-signal for its intended purpose, to pinpoint specific actions as they're taking place.

When the whales at Sea World are taught to do "bows" where they jump out of the water and dive back in headfirst, the trainers bridge them when the whale is reaching the top of his arc. Bridging at that moment draws attention to the action of going up in the air. If the whales were given a bridge-signal when they entered the water after performing the bow, they would try to get back in the water faster, thinking it was the act of getting back into the water that was the desired behavior. In that case, the bows would get lower and lower as the whales tried to hasten their return to the water. It's important to pinpoint the action you want repeated and to time your bridge-signal accordingly so that it's clear that you're bridging the precise behavior you want repeated.

I met a woman who was trying to use reward-reinforcement without using a bridge-signal. She was attempting to teach her young mare to lift her legs so she could pick out her feet. The woman couldn't understand why her horse wasn't learning the lesson she was trying to teach. She reported that she would feed her mare every time she finished picking a hoof. Instead of cooperating, the young horse was pulling her foot away and putting it on the ground. The mare pulled her foot away for a good reason. Since she got reinforced each time her foot was set back down, that was the action she was repeating. She was just trying to perform the action she believed was getting her fed. If this woman had been using a bridge-signal, she could have bridged when the horse's hoof was still in her hand. Even though she would still feed her mare after the foot was back on the ground, she would have effectively communicated through the bridge-signal that allowing the foot to be held was the desired action. The horse remembers the action that gets bridged. The adage that "timing is everything" really applies here.

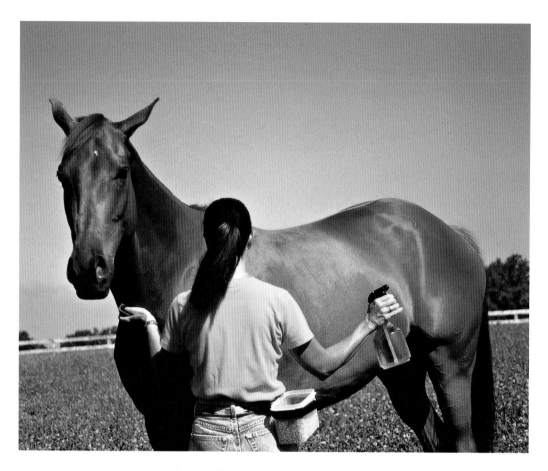

I'm teaching Mint to accept the fly spray. In this photo I'm actually spraying away from him to get him used to the noise. I bridge with the clicker every time he doesn't react to the sound. Next, I will aim the spray at his body.

Sometimes, the action you want is actually lack of action. Suppose you want to teach your horse to stand quietly to be sprayed with insect repellent. Under that circumstance, you would bridge your horse for not moving when he's sprayed. He will get the idea that standing still and ignoring the spray is the behavior you desire (photo 23).

USING A VERBAL BRIDGE-SIGNAL

After your horse has gained experience with the clicker and you have taught him some behaviors using this mechanical bridge-signal, you may want to make the transition to a verbal bridge-signal. There are times, both on the ground and under saddle, when it comes in handy to be able to bridge without holding a clicker. Once your horse learns the verbal cue, you may use either signal interchangeably, even within the same training session.

We use the word "okay" as our verbal bridge-signal. You can choose any word or sound. We don't use our signal in a conversational tone. Instead, we say it in a crisp, deliberate tone to catch the horse's attention more easily.

Conditioning a horse to a second bridge-signal is a simple pairing process. If you are going to use the word "okay," say "okay" right before you click. Your horse will hear the new signal and start to anticipate hearing the original bridge-signal next. After a few sessions, your horse will understand your new bridge-signal. Once he learns it, he will respond just as well to your verbal signal as he does to the clicker.

TARGET-TRAINING

The target serves an equally important function as a learning tool. Until this point in training, there have been few standards established for receiving reward-reinforcement. Now, we are ready to establish the relationship between working behavior and receiving reinforcement. Even if your goal for your horse is to improve his performance under saddle, you will still benefit by spending a few days target-training him. It will help you build a good working partnership. A horse enjoys the mental stimulation in these training sessions and seems to look forward to them. Target-training enhances the whole process. It teaches him the concept of earning reward-reinforcement in return for deliberate actions and sets the stage for more advanced learning. You will be teaching your horse to think and develop his problem-solving skills. In the sessions, the target serves as a focal point, something familiar and comfortable. After the initial training, a horse knows what to do when he sees the target. He develops a rein-forcement-history in association with the target. As his reinforcement-history expands, a horse will increase his efforts to please you. So take the time to target-train with this tool and expand your relationship.

We designed a target that's been very useful for starting horses in our system. It's made of a dowel, about two-and-a-half feet in length, with a marine float attached to one end (photo 24). The idea of using a target with such a distinct end is to help a horse discriminate between the han-

24   This is the target we use in our On Target work, and it is similar to the targets used at Sea World. You, however, can use your imagination and create your own target. The important thing is to have one end of the target distinctively different from the other.

dle end and the marine float (the target), which is the end we want him to touch with his nose. The most useful targets are those you can easily hold and move around.

When we begin target-training, there is one criterion. We want our horse to touch his nose to the target-end of the stick. Before you begin, think about what you want to accomplish in the initial target-training session. Accept and reward small steps that build toward your goal. The best place to start target-training is a controlled environment where your horse is comfortable, such as his stall. Enter his stall with the target, a container of food, and your bridge-signal. In this stage of training, your horse will be quite interested in your appearance in his stall. This interest will help toward your goal since the horse may touch the target out of curiosity. If this happens, even if it's clearly by accident, bridge and feed your horse right away. Even if the horse turns his head in your direction and his nose grazes the target in the process, bridge and reinforce this action, since it's the one you want. It doesn't matter how accidental the touch is as long as your horse meets the one criterion and touches the target.

Some horses may be more frightened than curious when first introduced to the target. If your horse is alarmed by this unusual looking object, hold the target very low and still and wait for him to move toward it (photo 25). As soon as the nervous horse takes a step or reaches toward the target, bridge and reinforce. You can build up to actually touching it, but to start, you can teach him to get nearer to the target. Again, the action you bridge is the action that you want repeated. If your horse approaches, but then backs away, don't bridge this behavior because you will be communicating that backing away is what you desire. If he approaches the target but you miss the opportunity to bridge and he backs away, don't bridge that behavior either. Don't be concerned, however, if your horse backs away after you bridge. By bridging, you are drawing attention to the action he is doing at

25   When target-training a skittish horse, begin the process crouching down. It makes both you and the target seem less intimidating. Horses are less likely to feel defensive when people, or objects, are lower down.

the instant of the bridge. It's not difficult to achieve a good sense of timing. Just when you think "good boy" to yourself, that's the time to bridge.

PAIRING THE TARGET WITH A CUE

Most horses quickly learn the concept of touching their noses to the target. After your horse has touched the target just a few times, you can add another element to your training session. You can pair the presentation of the target with a cue, which is called "putting the behavior under stimulus control." Start this right away. The sooner you add pairing the target with a cue, the faster your horse will associate the signal with an action. I use the word "target" as my verbal cue. I also point to the target. You can teach any cue you prefer. When you give the cue, the horse will start associating it with the desired behavior. In this case, I say the word "target," and he begins to associate my saying the word as his cue to touch the target with his nose. Using a cue in this way is similar to pairing the bridge-signal with the presence of food. The cue "target" is paired with the presentation of the target. As you say "target," you will slowly raise it and hold it out for the horse to touch. When he touches the target, bridge and reinforce.

At the beginning of his training, your horse may want to touch the target without being sent to it. This is called anticipation and is both normal and helpful in the early stages. The first few times he does this it is acceptable, but once he seems comfortable and consistent with touching the target, you need to slowly make the criterion stricter. He needs to pay more attention to you, the trainer. It's important to teach him to stay with you and ignore the target until you send him. You don't want to spoil his good attitude so try to set him up to succeed by making the behavior you want clear to him. If he touches the target without getting a cue, respond with a three-second pause after he stops touching it. This will communicate to him that he's not going to be reinforced for that action. The objective of any training program should be to teach your horse to be attentive, responsive, and patient. He should be listening to you for what to do next. By establishing this early, you will help to curb your horse's anticipatory behavior.

Most horses, including our own horses, do something called "soliciting." They want to be reinforced and they want our attention. This is a good sign since it indicates enthusiasm for the new training program. However, it can get out of control when the horse offers the behaviors that have previously been reinforced without being asked to do so. Usually, he will perform the newest behavior in his repertoire because it has the most recent reinforcement-history. An under-saddle example might be teaching the horse to bend to the right. If you bridge and reinforce some approximations to the right, your horse will start wanting to bend to the right all the time because he is reinforced for this exercise. So be sure to balance it out by also bridging and reinforcing left bends and for going straight. In the process you will motivate him not just to bend to the right, but to listen to you under all circumstances. However, don't be surprised or overly concerned when you train your horse to do something and he wants to perform this action all the time. We need to teach him instead to focus his energy in a more constructive manner by performing the behaviors we ask of him. Simply teach him something new. Reinforce other behaviors as well. Both solicitation and anticipation can be curbed by responding with the three-second pause.

During this early stage, you are likely to be bridging and reinforcing your horse for staying with you and ignoring the target as often as you are bridging and reinforcing him for going to the target when you ask. At this point, you are establishing the stimulus control, which is the cue. In the presence of the stimulus, which is the word "target," your horse should touch the target. Otherwise, he should ignore it or be ignored.

MORE CHALLENGING TARGET LESSONS

When the early target-training lessons have been accomplished, it's time to increase the level of difficulty by asking your horse to touch the target in different locations. Hold the target out with your left hand, your right hand, lower it toward the ground, and then raise it slightly over your head (photos 26–29). Raising the target can, however, be intimidating to your horse. I've seen very few horses react comfortably the first few times the target is held over their heads, but they do learn that this is not threatening to them. If your horse has problems with this, go back a step or two and vary the placement less. When he is succeeding again, slowly try these new positions until he's comfortable with them.

The hand-held target is an extension of the hand and gives us more reach. Horses can also be somewhat desensitized to hands since they see them quite often. We don't always want them to touch our hands. Horses come to recognize the hand-held target immediately. It seems to retain more value for them.

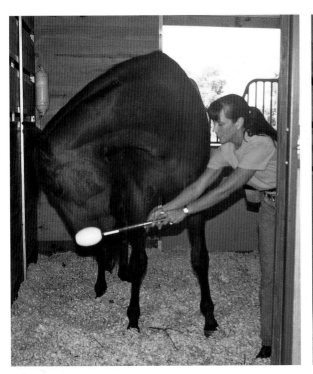

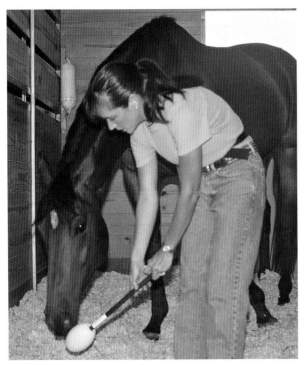

26-29   After your horse is comfortable touching the target right in front of his nose, present it in different locations so he has to reach for it. When he does, this indicates that he is learning that you want him to follow the target.

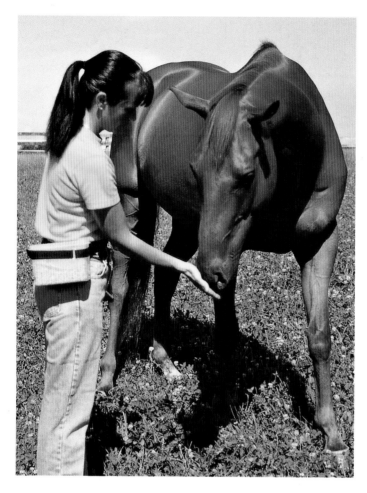

30   In this picture, I'm using my hand as the target and Mint is touching it. Although you should always start with a hand-held target, it's useful to teach your horse about your hand as a target later on so you can use it when a hand-held target is not available.

Using your hand as a target is another variation of the same theme. Instead of holding an object in your hand for your horse to touch, your hand becomes the object you want him to touch. Instead of saying "target," I usually use the horse's name as a verbal cue with a hand target. This teaches them the additional lesson of name recognition. Say your horse's name and present your open hand as the target, keeping fingers and thumb together to form a flat surface. The correct response is your horse touching his nose to your hand and holding gently on it (photo 30). Bridge and reinforce correct responses. Initially, you may even bridge your horse when he looks in your direction upon presenting the hand target. An intermediate step would be for him to walk toward you.

These steps should take about the same amount of time as it takes to bridge-condition. As with bridge-conditioning, a good guideline is four days with two five-minute sessions each day. You may find that this time frame serves to slightly overtrain the lessons, but it will build up a strong foundation for solid progress down the road.

Next in the process, it may help to affix the hand-held target to make it stationary; put the stick through the bars of a stall or gate. Then you can move around the stall with him and bridge and reinforce his attention toward you. Once you accomplish this, you can step close to the affixed target, point to it with your finger, and say "target." When your horse touches his nose to the target, bridge and reinforce, and then repeat the process a few times (photos 31 and 32). At first, your horse could get confused because the target is no longer attached to your hand. Point to the float end of it, even tap on it. As he touches it, bridge and reinforce. Continue in this manner. As he gets the idea, begin to send him to the target from distances slightly further away and eventually from different parts of the stall until he will go to it from any area. You may then permanently attach a target in a stall, paddock, or on a trailer.

Start by holding the new target in your hand and have your horse touch his nose to it. Bridge and reinforce him for a correct response. Then, attach the target. Stand next to it and say "target," or perhaps tap the target if this worked when teaching him to touch the fixed target in the early stages of training. When your horse touches the stationary target, bridge and reinforce him. Then, back away and send him from different areas of the stall. Next, give the cue from outside the stall with the door open. Eventually, send him to touch the target from outside the stall with the door closed.

Once the targeting-behavior is consistent and under stimulus control, increase the length of time that he touches the target. We do this in **successive approximations,** small building blocks that teach a new behavior. You can compare this teaching process to teaching a child to read. You start with the letters of the alphabet and then apply those lessons to teaching simple words and sentences. The next step might be a simple picture book, with many intermediate steps before the student is prepared to read complicated texts.

"Successive approximations" is a methodical, step-by-step process to build your horse's repertoire of behaviors. By breaking down the process into small steps, you progress in a positive manner, communicating which behavior you want every step of the way. In this manner, we have taught complex chains of behavior. Sometimes, these steps are assimilated quite

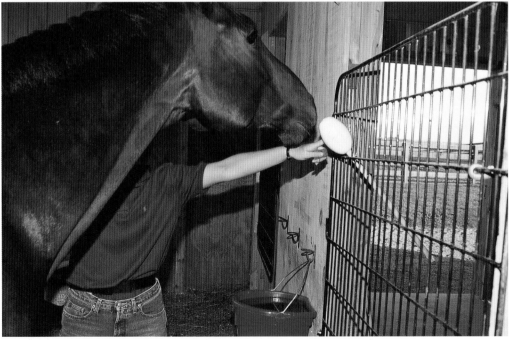

31-32   With clicker in hand, Erika is cueing Boomer by pointing to the target placed between the bars of the stall. As soon as Boomer touches the target, she will click and reward.

quickly. Other times, it takes longer, depending on the horse. When you train using successive approximations, you establish a foundation to return to should your horse not seem to understand what you are asking during the training process. Using the steps you've already trained him through, you refresh your horse's memory, get him back on the right track, and help to eliminate some frustration (photos 33 and 34).

We use successive approximations all through training, including the next step in target-training: lengthening the time the horse touches, or holds on, the target. Until this point, we have taught our horse simply to touch the target. By asking him to touch it longer, we add a dimension to the criteria. Increasing the holding time to one second would be a start. Send your horse to the target using the cue. Count to yourself for a second. If he remains touching the target, bridge and reinforce, repeat a few times, and then progress to two seconds, three seconds, and then five seconds. If your horse holds on the target for five seconds, I would conclude the training session. Especially through these early stages, it's best to keep the sessions short and pleasant. You will be able to slowly build the length and complexity of the sessions.

If your horse does not hold the target when asked to and moves away, give him a three-second pause and send him right back. Just before you think he might come off, give him the cue again. Point to the target and say "target." If he comes off his target but goes right back, bridge and reinforce this action. It shows he was thinking and made the correct decision. However, only bridge this behavior a few times. You don't want to inadvertently reinforce a **superstitious behavior.** Remember, this type of unintentional behavior can become part of the animal's repertoire when it is reinforced. Your horse could begin to think that the behavior sought includes going to the target, coming off the target, and then going back to the target. What you want is for him to hold on the target without breaking away. (More than likely, he will figure out that it is easier just to hold continuously than to come off the target and go back.)

If you are teaching your horse to target and he lifts a leg while touching it, be aware of this behavior. It's not a big concern if he does it a few times, but make sure you are not consistently reinforcing the leg-lifting. Your horse may believe that the leg-lifting is part of what you are asking. Instead, reinforce your horse when he touches the target without lifting his leg. By being aware and only reinforcing intended behavior, you avoid reinforcing superstitious behaviors.

33-34 In the first photo, I'm cueing Hershey to start a spin and Vinton is holding the target at the half-turn stage where Hershey will be rewarded. Once he reaches Vinton, I cue Hershey by calling his name and using my hand as a target. As he turns toward me to complete his spin, I bridge and reinforce. This is an example of how we use targets to teach a more complicated action, and how we break down the spin into steps.

An invaluable quality of the target, whether it is hand-held or stationary, is its familiarity as well as its mobility. You can use the target anywhere your horse goes, inside or out (photos 35–37). Once your horse has
been target-trained, he knows what to do with the target. With it, he will
develop a strong reinforcement-history, just as Husker Du, the jumper I
described in the first chapter, did.

Once your horse is trained to target, the varieties of ways you can use
this technique are endless. With a target, our horses have learned all sorts
of behaviors including stable manners, performance techniques, and
entertaining behaviors. They learned to load into trailers, stand still for
clipping, and lead, as well as back up, spin, lie down, and even jump over
fences (see photos 33 and 34). The upcoming chapters will show you how
to use On Target Training to teach your horse to be a better partner.

35-37 In this sequence I am teaching Mint to go to a target fixed to the fence in his paddock. While he is turned-out I ask him, by pointing and saying the word "target" and then taking a step in the target's direction myself, to go over to it at the fence. He makes the correct decision, walks to the target and holds on it until he hears the bridge-signal that signifies the end of a "behavior," or action. Notice he is listening for this signal so he can come to me for his reward.

WHEN TO END A TRAINING SESSION

Each interaction with your horse should feel like a fifty-fifty partnership. Your horse should be trying as hard as you are. Try to keep your sessions short and successful. The way to get his attention is by reinforcing him generously and quitting while he's still interested. When working on the ground, early sessions should span about five minutes and can increase commensurately with his level of training. Usually, you want to end the session while he still wants to spend more time with you. If you ask for too much too soon, your horse will want to quit out of frustration. Be sure to keep each session engaging and successful, particularly when training something new. As you train, you raise the criteria and ask more from your horse all the time. As he gives you a little more, reinforce him handsomely for his cooperative effort and attitude. The training sessions will then continue to grow in length and complexity.

There will come a time when your horse won't try or will persist in making the wrong decision. You'll try taking steps back to get him on track to no avail. Don't be discouraged by this plateau. This is also part of the learning process. Your horse is learning what happens when he does the wrong thing. Utilize the three-second pause. This consistent response will teach him that the incorrect behavior won't get him what he wants. When you are doing a session on the ground and you feel he is not trying or paying attention, terminate the session by walking away, leaving the paddock, or taking him home without reinforcement. Reward-reinforcement is in fact very rewarding. By walking away, you eliminate the opportunity for reinforcement. Many horses get frustrated when their trainers walk away under these circumstances. However, it is a necessary disciplinary action. Leave for five or ten minutes. Ignore your horse's tantrum or antics if he displays any. Reacting or returning to him when he has a tantrum could reinforce this behavior. Begin working again when you are ready and he is calm. If he still doesn't try, put him away and resume in an hour or two. Take a step back if you have to and only reinforce a small amount until you see his attitude come around. You are always teaching attitude and the last thing you want is for your horse to become complacent or quit. You want a horse with "heart." When he tries hard, do everything you can to be reinforcing. When he doesn't, terminate the session without getting emotional. Horses have off-days just as we do. Be patient and he'll get the right idea.

When you find yourself in the same position under-saddle, don't put your horse away. Your under-saddle sessions should be longer than the groundwork sessions. If you put him away each time he exhibits a bad attitude, he might learn to behave in an irritable manner, just to avoid work. Instead, continue to work, perhaps even step up the work level. However, if he seems to be having difficulty with an under-saddle exercise that he routinely does, don't push the issue. Instead, work on something else for a while and come back to the work he had a problem with later in the same session or the next day. If your horse continues to have trouble and you're sure it's not a physical problem, take a step back in training. Perhaps revisit some of the approximations you took to initially teach him the behavior in question. Set him up to succeed. During the training process, remember to remain calm. If you get tense, it can make your horse nervous and be counter-productive to progress.

TRAINING STRATEGIES

Every horse is capable of being trained using the On Target Training system. However, each horse has individual traits that will result in different responses during the learning process. We may recognize and anticipate some of these responses, but some may crop up unexpectedly. There are too many variables to count on the process going exactly as planned. That's why it's important to be flexible and willing to adapt On Target Training to your particular situation, keeping in mind that there is a solution to every stumbling block. It's just a matter of figuring out the best one for you. Start training by mapping out small steps toward achieving your goal. Then break those steps down even further. Remember that your horse's attitude is more likely to remain cooperative when you work him in shorter sessions and spread the progression of steps over a longer period of time. In the beginning, look for the smallest hint of progress toward your goal and bridge that action. Keep in mind that the action you bridge and reinforce is the action your horse will repeat. For example, suppose you are teaching your horse to load into a trailer. You're standing at the ramp with him and he bends his knee. I would bridge and reinforce this action because bending the knee is the first step toward lifting the leg, which leads to walking on to the ramp and ultimately into the trailer. In this case, bending the knee is the type of small action you should draw attention to with the bridge-signal.

When working with your horse, never underestimate the importance of standing still. Teach and reinforce this behavior quite often.

If your horse seems slow to learn or quits easily, set him up for success by reducing your expectations and mapping out smaller steps for him to accomplish. Reward each approximation with more food. Try shorter sessions. Once his attitude improves and he's motivated to try, you'll be able to move toward achieving your goal. Another situation you may encounter is the horse who tries initially and then stops making an effort. In this circumstance, back up a few steps and slow down while drawing attention to each effort he makes. If you've taken these steps and your horse is not improving, terminate the session. When your horse won't try, he chooses at that time not to be a part of the work session. It may take a few repetitions to teach him the ramifications of your leaving (his opportunity for reinforcement leaves with you), but ultimately he will learn to pay more attention to you.

Don't let these situations discourage you! They are part of the learning process and you will get past them as long as you are consistent in putting the tools in your arsenal to use. In some of these situations, the horse is testing or trying to control his environment. If he learns that his behavior won't get him what he wants, he'll change and stop being obstinate. Once you get your horse in the right frame of mind, his performance will improve.

REINFORCEMENT SCHEDULES

When you're ready to advance your training or raise your criteria for reinforcement, it's important to look at the subject of **schedules of reinforcement.** Psychologists have studied this issue in depth and discovered that if you reinforce every correct performance of an already trained behavior, the performance level decreases. But, feeding or reinforcing a trained behavior less predictably will increase the performance level. So, when you start training, for the first few weeks you should reinforce nearly every time you bridge—known as a fixed schedule of reinforcement—and immediacy of reinforcement is essential. You may start to implement a varied schedule of reinforcement after the first few weeks. There are many types of varied schedules, but we've found the most useful to be somewhat random.

Trainers of marine mammals have noticed that when animals have been reinforced on a predictable schedule, their efforts vary enormously. If they are only reinforced on every fifth "bow" (a movement where whales jump out of the water, arc, and then enter again head first), you can see the whales start their series of bows with less energy and vigor, only escalating their performance as they get closer to the fifth bow.

The answer with whales (and horses) is to change the frequency pattern of reinforcing certain actions and vary it to keep the animals trying harder all the time. The only exception to this rule is when you are teaching a new behavior, or action. This is the time to keep a more regular schedule of reinforcement, until the behavior is learned.

I like to vary what I feed, how much I feed, and how often I feed. Sometimes I have carrots, sugar cubes, and grain in my bucket so the horse I'm working with doesn't know what he'll get next. Sometimes I feed a small handful, and sometimes I feed several handfuls, or even all I have left in my bucket. Sometimes I will bridge and offer something besides food as a reward, keeping in mind what a particular horse enjoys, such as a scratch on the withers. Sometimes I bridge and just move on to another behavior. When I am training something new and subsequently raising criteria, I try to feed a higher percentage of the time, perhaps for eighty to eighty-five percent of my bridges. Once the behavior is trained, I would estimate I use a food-reinforcement sixty percent of the time. Remember, though, that when you train a familiar behavior in a new place, it may seem like training a new behavior, so feed accordingly.

When you raise criteria by implementing a varied schedule of reinforcement, reinforcement-history plays an important part. Let's say you teach your horse to lift his leg when you point to it. You have reinforced this consistently. (You should always focus first on the thought process and then turn to raising criteria.) At this point your horse has a solid understanding of what to do when he is asked to lift his leg and does so, but not with much effort. Now, you can make the task harder. You give him the cue and he raises his leg the usual small amount. This time, you may bridge, but not reinforce. Your horse anticipated a reward, but he didn't get one. He has a strong reinforcement-history with this behavior, which will cause him to try harder next time. You should bridge all extra effort and reinforce him.

You can also raise criteria or shape behavior through selective bridging, that is, only bridging the higher standard of performance. Raise criteria in small increments, using successive approximations. Remember to continue to set your horse up to succeed. Suppose you are teaching your horse to free-jump and you want him to jump higher. You are probably going to have more success if your horse is not tired. I wouldn't suggest riding your horse hard for an hour, dismounting, and then working on the new, harder level. Try the higher jumps when your horse has more energy. Conversely, if you've been working up to clipping his ears and you're ready to try actually clipping an ear, I would probably attempt that next step when he'll be the calmest, perhaps after he's been ridden or turned out.

Many of the aerial behaviors you see at Sea World are taught similarly. The jumps and back-flips are initially taught with a target, but the behavior is shaped and fine-tuned with selective bridging. When sea lions first learn a back-flip, it looks nothing like the finished behavior. It's like teaching a horse to jump. You start by teaching him the concept, and later he becomes adept at going back and forth over the fence. Then, let's say you want him to jump with his front legs tucked evenly or his back rounded. To accomplish this, you concentrate on bridging only those times that he jumps closer to the form that you are looking for. That's how he will begin to perform the behavior, just as much of the aerial behavior at Sea World is shaped. Initially, there is no finesse, but through the use of the bridge, you can refine style and performance.

CHAPTER

Practical Ground Training

GETTING STARTED

Teaching a green horse whose human contact has been minimal requires a different perspective than teaching a more seasoned animal. However, the following training fundamentals will also be useful for working with more experienced horses with problematic behaviors. We use the same approach to teach or reteach a good, solid foundation built on trust and respect, whether the horse's demeanor is due to greenness, trauma, or bad manners. To establish and increase motivation and communication, you'll use the On Target Training tools we talked about in earlier chapters, the bridge-signal and the target, to create a strong reinforcement-history and a desirable association with the behaviors we teach our horses.

The length of time it takes to shape behavior depends on the individual horse and his situation. If your horse is a veteran who has developed undesirable habits, it may take more time to reteach him than to teach a green or inexperienced horse. Think of this as balancing a scale. An untrained horse usually starts at neutral and builds up to affirmative associations. However, even a green horse who may not have spent a lot of time around people may have already developed mechanisms for dealing with his environment. For example, he may be skittish, or very assertive and not mindful of you. In either circumstance, you must exercise patience. No matter what the horse's past experience has been, he will come around with this program.

Before you begin teaching your horse the steps in this chapter, com-plete the bridge-conditioning and target-training processes in Chapter Three. While you may want to focus on a major training goal now, it's more important to concentrate on the smaller steps, the **successive approximations.** These steps are your intermediate goals. As you start working toward achieving these goals, remember that horses are individ-uals and their thought processes and progress will vary. I will outline train-ing approaches, but ultimately you must gauge your horse's progress and adapt your plans accordingly. When you teach two horses to do the same thing, you'll find that each training experience is quite different. The more you teach, the more you'll learn, and the more proficient you'll become.

As you begin your program, remember these two simple but very important axioms that apply to each training session. First, be sure to set your horse up to succeed. If, for example, it's a mounted lesson and you're teaching a reluctant, yet experienced, horse to go forward, when you start working with him you may choose to wear spurs. (Be sure that your seat is secure enough, and your leg steady enough, to avoid jabbing your horse unintentionally.) This may make it easier for the horse to understand your request, make correct decisions, and behave accordingly. You will then expand your opportunities to reinforce good choices and increase the like-lihood of a repeat performance of the desired behavior. After the horse understands the concept you are teaching him, you can fade-out whatever you first used to set him up to succeed, such as the spurs.

The second axiom you need to apply in this program is to be sure to bridge the action you want to see repeated. If you want your horse to stand quietly, click when he is still. If you want him to follow you, click when he is taking steps toward you. The action you bridge is the action you will see repeated.

The following training exercises are offered without a definitive time frame to follow. However, as always it's best to keep your sessions short. Sometimes, when the work is going exceptionally well, do very little — perhaps two exercises — pour the rest of the feed into the feed bucket, and be done. In this program, you are shaping attitude and focus as much as you are training specific behaviors. When your horse behaves exception-ally well, you should be especially reinforcing.

For the first month, keep each ground session to between five and ten minutes, building up gradually from there. If you work this way, your horse's attention span will increase dramatically. On the other hand, if you start with sessions that are too long, fun and easy learning experiences can become tedious and frustrating. Increase the length of the sessions but remember to vary the time span and, on occasion, do short sessions with lots of food. Even when you have built training sessions up to thirty to forty-five minutes, vary the length to keep your horse guessing and his effort and motivation level high.

TEACHING TOLERANCE

My focus in this section will be on working with horses who have little or no human contact. Often, these horses are skittish or wary of people. Because of the earlier bridge-conditioning work and target-training, you've already made great strides toward gaining your horse's acceptance. He has learned that you are not dangerous or threatening. By the time you are ready to concentrate on desensitizing him to touch, you've laid the foundation for developing trust.

Remember that your horse will do things because of associations he has made already. At this point, you have begun to build a reinforcement-history by bridge-conditioning and target-training him. Because of this groundwork, your horse will look forward to seeing you. He will start following you in the paddock and will keep an eye on you in the barn.

Next, I recommend you teach him to allow you to touch him all over his body, first with your hands, and ultimately with foreign objects such as a towel, lead rope, or stethoscope. You are training tolerance. This process is called desensitization. You want to desensitize him to humans, first and foremost. Once you establish this trust, you will introduce him to new objects.

For a variety of reasons, your horse should calmly accept your touch all over his head and body. You want your horse to stand quietly when you groom, when you examine him, when you treat him for injuries, and, eventually, for putting on tack. With the training foundation you have developed by bridge-conditioning and target-training, your horse should, at the very least, be comfortable with your presence. Your horse may also be comfortable being touched; however, I still recommend the tactile-tolerance training. Don't take good behavior for granted. By using the opportunity early in the training process to reinforce tactile acceptance, doing things later like caring for a sensitive wound or trimming hair around the

38-39 JD was a particularly timid foal—four months old here—when I was first introduced to him. He had just been weaned and was very nervous around people and I knew I had to build-up his trust before I could begin any work with him. It took me a week to get to the stage shown in these photos where he is letting me touch and reward him.

ears with clippers will be easier. You will be glad you took the time to firmly establish his trust.

The first goal is to have the horse stand still while you move around him, running your hands over his back, flanks, belly, chest, down his legs, and then over his neck, ears, and face. Some horses will be very wary and require more time to accept touching. Let's break the process into small steps.

Start working with your horse where he is comfortable, perhaps in his stall or paddock. I have found most horses like being touched first in the shoulder region, but of course preferences can vary. Determine where on his body your horse most easily accepts your touch and begin there. Initially, bridge and feed each time you touch him. Remember, it's

important to bridge the action you want repeated, so bridge while your hand is actually on your horse. This way, he will look forward to being touched. If you bridge when you remove your hand from his body, you will accomplish the opposite effect. He will soon find ways to avoid your touch so he can get fed more quickly.

Your horse may be a little nervous when you begin. Ultimately, the goal is to get him to stand quietly and relaxed. For now, you have to accept smaller steps and lower criteria. Bridge and feed the first few touches, then look for small improvements. Relaxation would be the first improvement, since you are working on attitude as much as on specific behavior. When you see apprehension subside, be sure to bridge and reinforce this positive change. You are, after all, seeking to build trust during the training process.

Some horses may progress well through the steps of tactile tolerance with just the use of the bridge-signal and food. Others may learn faster if you add the target as a training tool. By giving them something familiar and safe like the target, you effectively set the more skittish horse up to succeed. If you want to use the target for tactile tolerance, start by asking your horse to touch his nose to the target. Then, move your hand toward him. Bridge and feed him during this process for standing quietly and not moving away from your hand or the target.

For a horse that's especially worried about being touched, start the desensitization process by teaching him to disregard the movement of your hand. As he focuses on the target, move your hand around without touching him. As his comfort-level increases, move your hand closer. Bridge and reinforce throughout this process. When your horse calmly allows you to touch him, move your hand back and forth. Again, you're looking for him to relax while you're doing this, and you should bridge and feed even slight improvements toward this goal.

Once your horse calmly accepts your touch on his shoulder, move on to the other regions of his body, including his back, flanks, and belly. When you touch these new areas, remember to bridge and reinforce him for quietly allowing this. Continue the process until he stands in a quiet, relaxed manner as you move around his entire body to touch him. Keep bridging and feeding him for correct responses (photo 40).

If your horse has trouble standing still while you move around him, back up a few steps and return to touching where he was most accepting, making your hand movement smaller. Bridge and reinforce correct responses. Sometimes what seems like a minor issue to you can seem like a huge deal to your horse. When that happens, it's best to take a step back and allow him time to adjust. By being patient, you allow your horse time to make up his mind and get comfortable at his own pace. An added benefit of this training approach is that the results are far longer lasting than if you force the issue, which means your training will be more effective. Once your horse gets the initial concept, the training process will move along faster. Keep the sessions short and positive and remember to bridge and reinforce the small steps toward your larger goal.

Next, I'll focus on object-desensitization. The process will be the same as it was for tactile tolerance. The difference is you'll be teaching your horse to accept and be comfortable with being touched by unfamiliar objects. It's best to begin with something that seems benign, like a soft brush. If you begin with an object that's loud, large, and noisy like a plastic garbage bag, you could frighten even an older, seasoned horse. Before you begin, you might want to let your horse investigate the object with his nose, especially if he seems somewhat wary. Start at the area of his body

40   Here is Hershey allowing me to stroke his ears (see photo 9 for his previous reaction!). I reached this stage by taking it slowly and patiently, one step at a time. I started at the base of his neck with my desensitization techniques and worked my way toward his ears. Notice how relaxed he is now.

where he's most comfortable being touched, perhaps on his shoulder, just as you did when you initiated tactile desensitization. Touch him with the brush, then bridge and reinforce him. Take the same steps you did with your hand until you can touch him all over, including his face and neck. (Be aware that some horses may be nervous as you approach their faces.)

41-42 I'm showing George the towel before I rub him with it. Even though he is used to the towel, I still take this opportunity to reinforce his correct behavior of standing still in the paddock when he could easily walk off if he wanted.

When your horse stands quietly and is relaxed about being touched with the brush, repeat the process with a towel or lead rope. Try changing the locale for tactile object-desensitization sessions once your horse is consistently comfortable with being touched by various objects. You may have to take a step back in the training when you change the environment or even the session time. With new distractions and a change in the routine, your horse may be less focused in the beginning. Remember this is normal. At the end of the tolerance-training process, you should be able to approach your horse from either side, anytime, anywhere, and be able to touch or examine him without upsetting or frightening him (photos 41 and 42).

HALTER-TRAINING AND LEADING LESSONS

The initial goal in halter-training is to be able to place the halter on the horse's head without frightening him. Before you begin, be sure you have chosen a halter that fits correctly. If it's too tight, it will be difficult to get on and off and could hinder the learning process. If it's too loose, it won't be an effective training tool. Choose the type of halter you prefer. It may be one that slips over the ears and latches at the throat or goes over the poll and threads through a buckle. In this narrative, I am using a halter that slips over the ears and snaps at the throat. The training should begin by desensitizing the horse to the halter. Complete the steps in the previ-

43-45 Notice how Mint lowers his head to receive the halter in the first photo. I achieve this result by bridge-reinforcing him every time the halter is put over his nose. I also reward when the halter goes over his ears—a common problem area for horses—and then at the end if he makes the haltering experience an easy and pleasant one.

ous section and be sure your horse has become comfortable with having his head and ears touched, with both your hands and other objects, before you start.

First, your horse needs to get accustomed to the presence of the halter (photos 43–45). Then you can start the process of putting it on him. At first, hold the halter in position to slip it on his head and slowly raise it to his face with the noseband open. I recommend standing to the left side and facing the same direction as the horse to introduce this process. Standing directly in front of the horse can be a dangerous place. He could use his front legs to protect himself should he become frightened. Bridge and reinforce him when he remains still while the halter is near his muzzle, which will communicate to him that this is the desired behavior.

Repeat this step until your horse seems relaxed and comfortable. Next, slip the noseband over his muzzle. Bridge and reinforce him as he allows this so that he's being rewarded for each successful approximation. If he seems relaxed at this stage, feed him while the halter is over his muzzle. After he eats, take it off and do it again.

At this point, he's learning that every time the halter goes over his nose, he gets fed and again when it comes off. Once he understands this procedure, put it on the rest of the way. In the beginning, keep the halter a little loose so it doesn't feel too restrictive. When he allows you to slip the halter on all the way over his ears, bridge and reinforce him. Feed him a few handfuls when the halter is on and take it off after he eats. Repeat the process until he's comfortable wearing the halter. At the start of the next few sessions and feedings, slip the halter on and let him acclimate to the feeling of wearing it. The idea of connecting the wearing of a halter or other new equipment with food is that the horse will associate the halter going on his head with feeding time. This helps us build a desirable reinforcement-history. However, if your horse still shows a good deal of reluctance, back up a bit and build up his confidence using the earlier steps. Be patient and he will come around.

The next step, once your horse comfortably accepts putting on, taking off, and wearing his halter, is attaching the lead rope. Before you attach it to his halter, make sure your horse is comfortable with the lead. He should allow you to rub him all over his body with it. If he is reluctant, repeat the desensitization-steps discussed earlier in the chapter. Usually, at this stage of the training process, your horse will have built up a trust in you, his partner, and with his environment.

When you are ready to start teaching your horse to lead, recall the axioms we discussed earlier. Think about what you can do to set your horse up to succeed. One possibility is to work in a small area, such as in a stall or barn aisle. In case he is startled, he will be less inclined to run. However, if he lives in a field and you've done all the training there, he'll probably be most comfortable in the field. If that's the case, try to work in a small area or corner.

Before you teach your horse to lead with the rope, work on following the target (photo 46). Stand on your horse's left side. Hold the target to your right side and ask him to touch it with his nose. Bridge and feed the correct response. Next, take a step, then two, until he is walking and then turning with you. Also work on stopping. When you stop, I suggest introducing the word "whoa" or a cue that you choose to mean stop. Say the word just before you stop. At first, your horse will stop because you and the target stopped. Soon, though, he will learn what the word means, and when he hears it, he'll know you and the target are about to stop.

After these lessons are accomplished, you can begin fading-out the target. When your horse learns to walk with you, drop the target by your side. It's actually an easy transition to make since it's easier to follow your movements than to follow and touch his nose to the target. When he is walking with you on his left side without the target at nose-level, bridge and reinforce every few steps. Work on him turning and stopping with you. As he understands the new criteria, reduce the number of times you bridge.

46   When being lead with a halter and lead rope, JD, the four-month-old weanling, had learned to follow other horses, but was extremely difficult and reluctant to go on his own. I dealt with this situation by starting him with On Target Training basics (even at his age) and progressed to having him follow the target into the paddock without a halter. Soon thereafter I was able to lead him normally. I always advise horse owners to start the On Target Training process as soon as their foals are weaned.

At this point, he should be ready for the lead rope. Attach the rope and use the target to teach him to stay with you. Since you're adding a new factor in the equation, the familiar target makes it easier for him to succeed. Also, drawing his attention to the target reduces his focus on the rope. As soon as you attach the rope to his halter, ask him to target before he has time to think about the rope. When he touches the target, bridge and feed. Now that you've added the weight of the lead rope, go back to bridging and reinforcing the smallest steps again. The feel of this extra equipment may not seem like a big deal to us, but to our horses it could seem monumental. Don't take his cooperation for granted. If your horse is comfortable with these steps, it will be apparent. You may be able to move quickly through certain phases of this training. Other phases may require more time and patience. Build up to walking, turning, and stopping, using the target as his focus.

There should be no pressure from you pulling on the rope at this stage. You want your horse to walk with you and also to respond correctly to the pressure of a lead rope and halter. The first time he feels that pressure, more than likely he'll pull back. This is an instinctive response. (Dogs usually do this their first time on a leash.) This is where a small working-space can be an advantage since this will minimize a horse's inclination to flee. You may get through walking, stopping, and turning using the target without your horse pulling on the rope. Or he may test the rope right away. Ideally, you'll be the one who initiates that phase of the training when the time seems right. When he seems comfortable with leading with the target, start acclimating your horse to the sensation of pressure from the lead rope. Start with gentle, forward pressure on the lead rope while walking with him. Present the target just ahead of him so he will voluntarily walk forward. Then click and reward.

Eventually, the lead-rope pressure will be simply a cue to move in the direction of the pressure. If he is very resistant and not paying attention to the target, the rope pressure and pulling should be gentle, but firm and constant. In this circumstance, you are teaching with removal-reinforcement. This is the traditional side of halter and lead-rope training. When he stops pulling on the lead rope, you relieve the pressure. Teach him that the pressure will go away when he stops pulling, even for a second. The tricky part of removal-reinforcement is that you need a well-developed sense of when to give. When he gives for a second, you give for a second. When he pulls you, you need to respond with an equal amount of pressure, but without jerking him, which could result in frightening or harming him and make the situation worse. Remember, the bottom line is even a young horse is stronger than a person. That's why supplementing traditional training with our system can help turn the odds in your favor. By adding the bridge-signal, you communicate more clearly. With the target, you can set your horse up to succeed, and there is something worthwhile in it for him. He'll get fed. With traditional methods, the only benefit your horse derives when he cooperates is not being pulled.

Your horse needs to learn that you want him to move forward when you gently put pressure on the lead rope. When you apply a bit of pressure with the rope or if your horse begins to pull, maintain the pressure on your end of the rope, hold the target in front of him, and ask him to touch it. As soon as reaches forward and he eases the pressure, bridge and feed. Touching the target adds a familiar element to the exercise. He understands that you are asking him to move forward and touch it. Thus, you are setting him up to succeed in achieving the lesson objective, which is to move forward in response to lead rope pressure. Focus on this response. At first, apply a forward gentle pull and present the target in front of him, keeping in mind the importance of softening the pull and bridging as soon as he responds correctly. Then, progress to walking forward. To introduce turning (once he has mastered moving forward), gently pull to one side or the other and present the target again. He will learn to discriminate the direction of the pressure.

Next, work on stopping by first using your word for stop and then applying some gentle pressure from the lead rope. Bridge and reinforce the small steps as you work with your horse. When he understands the concept you're teaching, reduce the number of times you feed. Next, fadeout the target and then fade-out the lead rope pressure. (Refer back to Chapter Two if you need a refresher on fading-out training tools.) Ultimately, your horse should walk, turn, and stop without contact on the rope or halter while also understanding what to do when tension is applied to the lead rope. Once your horse can do this well in a small area, move to new areas. Keep the sessions short when you do this. In a new area, your horse could become distracted, excited, or nervous. To help him gain confidence and focus in a new place, reintroduce the target again until he responds correctly. It's important to teach your horse that the same rules apply no matter what your environment or outside stimulus (photo 47).

TEACHING HIM TO CROSS-TIE

If you have been following the program so far and have taught your horse the bridge-signal and the target, and have done the tolerance-training and

47   I am leading JD toward a metal sculpture (in the photo). However, he balks when he sees it, so I use the target (without pulling on the lead rope) to help me get him closer. He follows the target and I bridge and reinforce him. He becomes confident about this particular "dragon," as well as bolder in general when faced with new experiences.

halter and lead-rope work, you are well on your way to establishing a strong, solid training base. Continue to build upon that foundation by teaching your horse to stand calmly on cross-ties and allow grooming and other necessary tasks.

Before we can put a horse on the cross-ties and expect him to stand quietly, it's helpful to teach him to stand quietly without being tied. Choose an area where your horse is comfortable and unlikely to be distracted. You may want to use a halter and lead rope for this work, although you won't use them as "correction" tools. They just make it easier to catch your horse if he wanders away.

First, come up with a cue that you want to use to ask him to stay (photos 48–50). I put both hands on one side of the horse's shoulder and barrel and say the word "stay." I then back away from his side and walk to his rear so it's easy for him to understand the difference between walking with me at his head and staying still with me behind him. Whatever you choose, make sure your cue is clearly different from any other. Stand at your horse's side with one foot slightly behind the other. Give the cue and move back from your horse's side, preferably the left side, by just shifting your body weight to the back foot. If he allows you to do this and remains where he is, bridge and reinforce. This is the first small goal toward the larger goal. Next, give your cue again and take a half step further back. If he responds correctly, click and feed. If he responds incorrectly, go back to your cue, such as placing your hands on his barrel and shoulder. If he remains still during your smallest movement away from him, bridge and reinforce. Continue to build on this process until he lets you walk around him. The benchmark I would suggest for this exercise is that he may not move his feet. I don't mind if he moves his head. However, it may be important to you that he holds his head still for an upcoming conformation class to give you one example. Reinforce the behavior you want to be repeated.

Once your horse understands the cue to stay, take him somewhere different, perhaps to the area where you plan to teach him to tie or cross-tie. To set him up to succeed with this behavior, you can begin working with him at a time of day he'll be most relaxed and most likely to stand still, perhaps after he has been turned out, hand-walked, or ridden. If you tried this first thing in the morning when he was expecting to go out with his friends who were just turned out, he could be restless or agitated. It's better to pick a time when you will have the most success. Later in the

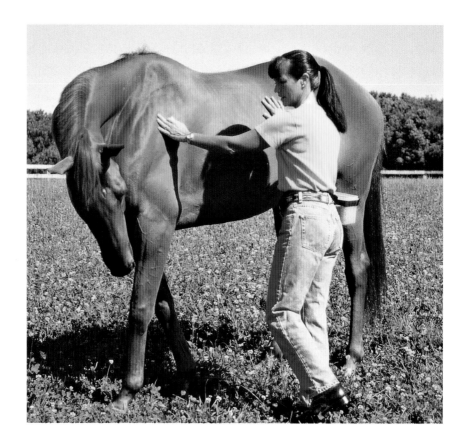

48-50   Teaching Mint to "stay." In the first photo I am giving him my cues: I put one hand on his barrel, the other on his shoulder, and ask him to "stay." Next, I rock back on my legs and take my hands off his body. If he doesn't move, I proceed to walk off behind him and bridge-reinforce. If he does move at any point, I go back one stage of the lesson and give my cues again.

training program, you'll be able to work this behavior anytime and anywhere. To begin though, you need to give yourself the chance to build up his reinforcement-history. If your horse walks away, ask him to target on your hand (I discussed this technique in detail in Chapter Three), or on a hand-held target. Then, move to his side and ask him to stay. Continue to bridge the incremental behaviors that lead toward the desired goal of standing still. Just as you did previously, build up until he is performing up to the standard you've set.

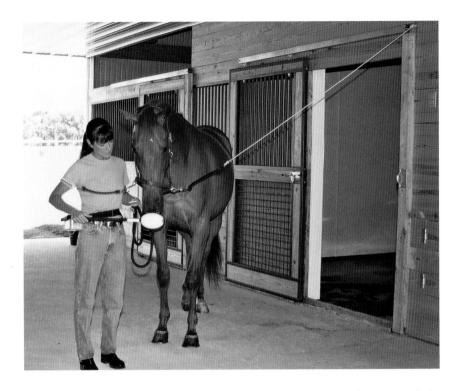

When you first introduce your horse to cross-ties, use the target to help take his mind off any pressure from the rope. When he relaxes and stands still, bridge and reinforce.

Once your horse stands quietly when asked and understands he should give in to the pressure of a lead rope, he's ready to learn about tying. Be sure to begin in a safe place with good footing. Avoid slippery surfaces. For added safety, I recommend using cross-ties that "give" or can be released quickly if a horse panics. With the lead rope still attached, hook the cross-ties to the halter. As soon as you do, place the target directly in front of him, close enough so that he can touch it without taking a step (photo 51). When he touches it, click and feed. Continue to bridge and reinforce each successful touch of the target, even if he seems somewhat nervous at first. Also bridge and reinforce every sign of relaxation. Usually, a horse will try to test this new restraint. When this happens, introduce the target just in front of him to alleviate the pressure the ties put on his halter. (You don't want to inadvertently teach him to lunge forward away from the pressure.) As soon as he gives in to the pressure, click and feed while he's still on the cross-ties. Then detach the cross-ties from his halter. This is a case where you use removal-reinforcement as a training aid. It is not just the pressure from the cross-ties that goes away when your horse gives in, it's the pressure of the whole situation that is removed, too.

Keep these initial sessions very short. However, if your horse is relaxed about being on the cross-ties, leave him on for longer increments asking him to stay with your cue and using the target to help him focus. He will concentrate on these familiar actions making his constraint on the cross-ties less of an issue.

In this training system, you allow your horse to make a decision giving him enough time to grow comfortable with a new situation. If, out of fear, your horse pulls back in panic, use gentle pressure on the lead rope to bring him forward again on the cross-ties. Do allow him some movement while cross-tied. He will relax more easily and this will go a long way toward building trust. Once your horse decides by himself to commit to a task that used to frighten him, he will perform it better, longer, and more readily than if he is forced into the same situation.

If your horse becomes very nervous, back up a step in the training process. Use the lead rope and target to get him focused. As soon as he settles even the slightest bit, unhook the cross-ties. Remember not to react strongly if he seems panicked. You can make him even more upset. Try to remain calm. Ask him to target and allow him a little more time to make a correct decision. He may perceive this situation as life-threatening and react accordingly. If so, he needs more time and patience to learn and trust that being on cross-ties is not threatening to him. You may need to start all over again and just use one cross-tie at first. You may even have to feed him when he allows the cross-ties near his halter without reacting. When you attach one cross-tie, bridge and reinforce when you can clip it on him without a fuss. Then, with plenty of slack in the cross-tie, ask him to target with his head toward the other cross-tie. This will put a slight amount of pressure on the cross-tie that's attached to his halter. Bridge and reinforce him for allowing this. Feed him with the cross-tie attached and end the session. Build on this beginning until you can replicate the sensation of being cross-tied on both sides using the lead rope as one of the cross-ties, building up this exercise until he stands quietly this way for a few minutes. The advantage to working with the lead rope acting as one of the cross-ties is that you can quickly release it if he panics. When he is coping with this well and seems comfortable, attach the other cross-tie. When attaching the second cross-tie, you raise the criteria, so remember to make things quick and easy for him again.

If your horse is brand new to cross-ties and reacts adversely, more than likely he is simply worried about his lack of freedom for flight. Over time, he will learn that he doesn't need to flee. However, an older, trained horse who panics in the cross-ties has usually had an unpleasant experience with them. You need to make it enjoyable. So if possible, put him on the cross-ties and feed him his dinner. This will do wonders for his confidence. For now, I suggest that while he is cross-tied, avoid doing things your horse doesn't like. Instead, hold him yourself with a lead rope for the vet or for clipping. Once he is completely comfortable with these procedures, then move him to the cross-ties. You should never ask your horse to do something while cross-tied that he is not comfortable doing just standing. This policy will help avoid further cross-tie problems and dangerous situations. You may train behaviors while your horse is cross-tied, but start with very small steps and keep the time frame brief. Building the behaviors slowly while he is cross-tied will keep your horse's comfort-level high and will develop a desirable reinforcement-history.

PADDOCK ABC'S

Turning a horse out or bringing him in seems to be a constant source of headaches for many people. Vinton and I are often asked questions concerning paddock and turnout-related issues. We've noticed that these essentially center around three concerns. First is excitability when walking to or from the paddock. The second is bolting when the handler is about to release a horse. The third is the horse refusing to be caught once turned out.

Let's begin this discussion with the first issue: controlling excitement while walking to or from the paddock. It's not unusual for horses to be eager for turnout since this is their opportunity to run, play, graze, and socialize. It's important that they have this chance to release energy and just be horses. However, horses must learn to contain their energy while working with people.

Your horse may be perfectly behaved being led anywhere except to and from the paddock. If this is the case, you need to incorporate training sessions when turning your horse out and when bringing him in.

52 This is the picture we all strive for when turning out and bringing in—a calm, alert but relaxed, horse with a happy handler!

Jigging or trotting without being asked can easily escalate into worse behavior such as bucking or rearing, so it's best to nip this in the bud before it gets to a more dangerous level. I recommend using the target in these exercises, just as you did when you taught your horse to lead. Using the target helps you set your horse up to succeed.

Before you begin the first session, notice where in the turn-out process your horse tends to begin losing his focus and self-control. Is it right away? Once he leaves the barn? Or does he begin to act up when he sees another horse? Just before the trouble point, give him something constructive to do. Start with some kind of reinforcement. Put a few carrots in your

53 Mint is charging up to the fence, something that frequently leads to George becoming excited. Here, however, George is choosing to listen to me, knowing that the carrots in my back pocket are there to reward him for being quiet.

pocket or scoop some grain into a waist pack or side-bucket. Gather up your clicker and target, too. At this point in the training process, your horse should be adept at bridge-conditioning and target- training, so this work should be quite familiar. Get your horse prepared for turnout as you usually do. Just as you step out of the stall with him, ask him to target, then bridge and reinforce the correct response. Take a few steps and ask him to target again.

Keep the location in mind where things usually begin to fall apart. Just before you get to that spot, while your horse is still behaving correctly, ask him to target. Then, bridge and reinforce the correct response. Continue going toward the paddock a few more steps and repeat the process, until you get to the paddock gate. If he is still behaving correctly, bridge and reinforce. Feed him a few handfuls as extra reinforcement before you release him into the paddock. (I discuss how to ensure an uneventful release soon.)

If your horse gets excited on the way, stop. Once he stands quietly, proceed toward the paddock. Continue asking him to target every few steps. It's fine to ask him to stop before asking him to target when you begin these sessions. Then, move up to targeting while walking, decreasing the number of times you ask him to target. Finally, remove the target from the training process and instead bridge and reinforce him for walking quietly toward the paddock. Always save extra feed for the successful completion of this task, which is getting to the paddock without incident. Feed less frequently along the way as he progresses and feed more when he arrives at the paddock without a problem having arisen. You may want to walk him out to the paddock and use his entire breakfast as reinforcement.

Consider your horse's eagerness to get to the paddock. Being turned out is reinforcing in and of itself. If he loses control on the way to the paddock and you stop him for several seconds until he is calm, you are removing one of his reinforcers, which is going toward the paddock. When he regains self-control, proceed at a nice, slow pace. When he behaves correctly, your horse not only gets to walk toward his reinforcement—the paddock—but he will also receive food as an additional reinforcement. He needs to learn that in order to go out, he must be courteous and respectful of his handler. If he is really uncooperative in the session, turn around and take him back to his stall for a few minutes before trying to turn him out again. Sometimes, this action has a bigger impact on his behavior than food-reinforcement. There are all types of reinforcements; by paying attention to what your horse enjoys and desires, you can increase your influence on his behavior.

If your horse gets excited on his way back to the barn after being turned out, employ the same tactics. If he isn't being reasonable about coming in, turn around and put him back in his paddock. Most likely, he will get a little anxious when you walk away. Ignore him for a few minutes and then return and try again.

Another big problem is the horse who bolts at the paddock gate or just before it. This behavior can be an escalation of losing control on the way there—the previous situation I discussed—and it can be very dangerous, not just for your horse, but also for you and anyone in the area.

Let's focus on this process of being released into the field at the gate. If your horse behaves best when he's the first horse to go out, when he goes out with another horse, when he's put in one specific paddock rather than in another, or if he's turned out after exercise, start one of these ways to set him up for success.

Begin these training sessions walking to and from the paddock. Use a target. Ask him to walk at a regular pace while targeting from time to time. Then, ask him to slow his walk quite a bit. This will get him to pay more attention to you. When he masters this exercise, you are ready to lead him into the paddock. First, ask your horse to target outside the paddock gate. Bridge and reinforce his correct response. Feed him only a small amount as reinforcement. Then, open the gate and enter slowly, being careful that your horse doesn't sense and react to any excitement or wariness on your part. As soon as you accomplish this, ask him to target. When he does, bridge and reinforce. When you reinforce, dump the rest of the feed or treats on the ground for him to continue eating. Remove the lead rope and halter (if you usually take the halter off), close the gate, and walk away.

If your schedule permits, repeat this exercise several times a day, to help take away some of the novelty of being turned out. Also, you may have more success if he has already been turned out that day, since he will probably feel less excited. Get your horse's attention by repeating the session at mealtime, using his food as reinforcement to expedite learning. After you do this routine a few times, your horse will begin to anticipate that he may get fed if he behaves correctly inside the paddock gate. Bridge and reinforce him for walking patiently with you on the way to the paddock. However, feed him the largest portion once he has walked calmly through the gate.

The third common paddock issue is catching your horse. I'll outline how to teach him to come when he's called. First though, you need to evaluate what is going on in the paddock when you want to catch him. Perhaps he is out with his friends nearby. He is grazing and enjoying the room he has to run and play in. Most horses find this environment very reinforcing. Then you enter the paddock to catch him and take him away from all this enjoyment, most likely to work him. In this scenario, is it any surprise that many horses are reluctant to be caught? To some horses, your arrival in the paddock can seem like an opportunity for a good game of chase. To teach your horse to come when called, you need to make it more reinforcing to come to you than to stay in the paddock.

When you begin this session, start with the hand-held target. He will see this from further away, which will help him to succeed with this final paddock-manners exercise. Enter the paddock, equipped with your hand-held target and side-bucket of feed. You may need to get close to your horse before he responds. Start by walking toward him. When he looks at you, call his name, present the target and keep walking toward him. Then, ask him to target again. Bridge and reinforce his correct responses. When your horse approaches, ask him to target. Bridge and reinforce the correct response. Repeat the sequence a few times, then turn and walk out of the paddock. If your horse follows you as you leave, bridge and reinforce him while he's walking with you but leave him behind in the paddock. He will most likely realize that he'll get reinforced for coming to you without necessarily being taken out of his preferred environment. If possible, repeat the sequence a few times a day to teach him that he will be reinforced for coming to you when called, and that the consequence of coming to you won't always be leaving the paddock.

Naturally, you will need to take him out of the paddock sometimes. Vary what happens when you bring him in. Sometimes, feed him when you bring him in. Sometimes, put him in his stall with hay for a while. Or, take twenty minutes or so and do anything with him rather than ride. This will keep him guessing about the reason he is leaving the paddock.

Breaking up the pattern your horse expects to follow goes a long way toward solving the "catching" problem. When he gets better about coming to you and leaving the paddock, put his halter on, lead him out of the gate, and then turn around, go back into the paddock and release him. You can release him back to the same paddock or put him in another one. Remember to reinforce him throughout this process.

As your horse becomes more willing to come to you when called, start fading-out the hand-held target. Instead, begin to use your hand as the target. Switch from feed in a side-bucket to a few carrots in your pocket. Do this to ensure that your horse will come over to you because he sees you, not necessarily because of what he sees you carrying.

HORSE CARE 101: GROOMING, VET, FARRIER, CLIPPING

When standing quietly on cross-ties becomes routine for your horse, you can begin teaching him to accept grooming, clipping and bathing, veterinary and farrier work, as well as injury or wound care. All of these routine procedures build from, and are variations of, object-tolerance and tactile-acceptance work that I discussed in the beginning of this chapter. In order to build a pleasant association with these procedures, begin your sessions in your horse's stall, proceed when he's relaxed to standing in the area where he'll be cross-tied, and then onto the cross-ties when he's ready.

When you start this work, your initial goal shouldn't be to groom him completely, or clip him, the first day. Instead, you want to begin teaching your horse what is desired of him. You want to help your horse become comfortable with each of these tasks. Down the road you will not have to feed him for everything you ask of him but for now, the frequent feeding is used as a tool to communicate approval to your horse and to motivate him to make the right decisions. Ultimately, your horse's training will go faster because he is trying harder to do the right thing. Keep the bigger goal in mind but take small steps along the way. Continue to keep your sessions short and positive when starting something new. Your progress will vary, depending on your horse and his history. Continue to plan how to set your horse up to succeed in each lesson you teach him.

• *Grooming and Clipping*

Grooming tasks consist of currying, brushing, picking feet, vacuuming, mane care such as braiding or pulling, bathing, and clipping, to name a few. For each task, you need to desensitize your horse to a new sensation. It could be tactile for currying and bathing, a new sound for clipping and vacuuming, or even a person working from a new place, like a step stool for braiding. Each new object needs to be introduced to your horse. When introducing grooming equipment such as brushes and curry combs, start with object-desensitization work in his stall until you can move each of these objects over his whole body. Among these pieces of equipment, the one that may be most problematic is the curry, since the feel of the curry comb is not always one horses enjoy. Many horses are sensitive to firm currying, especially on certain areas of the body. Start with light currying and gradually build up the pressure you apply. Bridge and reinforce your horse for standing still while you're working on him. Continue the process in small steps, building up until you can curry without much movement from him.

With vacuums, clippers, and bathing, there is more than one sensation to cope with. There is the tactile sensation of these objects touching him, as well as the noises they make, which you must teach the horse to ignore. I will focus on clipping as the example, since many horses have a difficult time adjusting to being clipped.

Most horses who have problems being clipped are sensitive around their ears. Whether your horse is being clipped for the first time or has spent a lifetime trying to avoid it, the steps will be the same. In most cases, the experienced horse will prove to be more trying when you teach these lessons. However, with time and lots of patience, you can improve his comfort level. Keep in mind that the seasoned horse has a strong rein-forcement-history; he may find clipping so dreadful that he will go to great lengths to avoid it. You need to rebalance the scales in favor of clipping. The novice horse, on the other hand, is more likely to be neutral about the whole process.

There are several factors that can make clipping uncomfortable. You can't control them all but you can teach the horse to be more stoic about the details of clipping that particularly trouble him. Also, through On Target Training, he will ultimately learn that it is more reinforcing to put up with this necessary procedure, even the aspects of clipping he finds most unpleasant, which are likely to center around his ears. He probably won't like it when shorn hairs fall into his ears; if they tickle or annoy him and he shakes his head, that motion can cause him to be jabbed by the clippers, causing further discomfort. There isn't much you can do to pre-vent this scenario other than teach the horse to stand still while this task is accomplished. A hand-held target for him to focus on might come in handy for this lesson (photos 54 and 55). While you work be as careful as possible not to accidentally poke him with the clipper blades. Before you begin, though, ascertain that the clipper blades are sharp. Dull blades can pull the hair and will increase clipping time since you'll need to make more passes over the same area. Because your horse's skin is sensitive, hot blades can also cause discomfort. Be sure to keep the blades lubricated and check them regularly to determine that they're not too warm.

Before you turn on the clipper switch, begin with object-desensitiza-tion. Start with the clippers unplugged and quietly stroke them over the body part your horse seems most relaxed about you touching. Build slow-ly in several sessions until he is comfortable with you rubbing the clip-pers all over his body. Next, plug them in and turn them on. At this point, your horse is likely to take a very different view of the clippers.

Hold the clippers (still running) in one hand while you do tactile-desensitization work with the other hand. As you move your hand to dif-

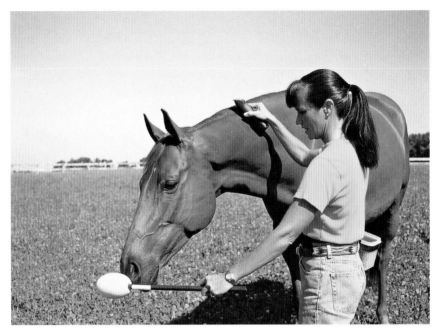

54·55 In the first photo above I'm preparing Mint for clipping by having him "target" while I hold the "buzzing" clippers on his neck. He responds well, so I bridge and reinforce. Then I move the target toward my body so he will follow it with his head thus making it easier for me to reach his poll.

ferent areas of his body and he responds correctly by remaining still or relaxing, bridge and reinforce. He may be anxious and jumpy at first, so build up gradually, looking for small improvements to start. When he allows you to touch him everywhere on his body while the clippers are running in your other hand, start bringing the clippers closer to him without touching him. Again, click and feed for even a minimally correct response. When you can bring the clippers very close to your horse and he remains calm, move to the next step.

Begin to touch your horse with the clippers turned on, but don't actually clip any hair yet. You are desensitizing him now to the vibration. Start on his body where he is most relaxed about being touched. Gradually move to other areas. This may go quickly or it may take a week or more. Don't fret over the time taken. When he is comfortable about being touched by running clippers all over his body including his head and neck, begin the process of clipping. Don't worry about doing a complete, or even an aesthetic, job at first. Instead, you want a good experience so clip the area where your horse feels most comfortable. You could start with one stroke of the clippers on a leg. Bridge and reinforce if he remains calm. Then you may want to try a stroke on his chin. Again, reinforce him if he exhibits the desired reaction. If the session went well, end it. In the next session, repeat the routine and add a stroke or two. Build on this process gradually. Slowly progress to the ears.

If your horse has serious problems with clipping, it may take quite a while until he trusts you enough to begin the clipping process. Use the target as an aid to encourage him to lower his head while mimicking clipping. Be patient and allow him the time he needs to make correct decisions. It may take a long time, but with patient perseverance, you will achieve your goal.

• *Sheath-Cleaning, Wound Care, and Foot-Soaking*
Much of the routine veterinary care you need to do with your horse can be accomplished with more trust and less stress after you've built up his reinforcement-history through this program. Care such as sheath cleaning, worming, injections, wound and injury treatment, and physical examinations is our next subject. These kinds of procedures have a common training approach, which is a variation of object-tactile tolerance.

When you approach the horse for sheath-cleaning or to care for a wound or injury, it's important to be aware of how sensitive he may be about these procedures. Injuries leave a horse feeling vulnerable. His innate tendency is to protect and even defend a wounded area of his body, and many horses also feel protective of their sheath area. So, you should take the same approach to desensitizing the horse to sheath-cleaning and wound treatment and make the same approximations toward handling both these sensitive areas. I'll discuss one—sheath-cleaning—with the understanding that you'll use the same process for both.

Before you begin approaching sheath-cleaning, complete the tactile-desensitization steps discussed at the beginning of this chapter. Your horse should also accept the other aspects of the procedure including the hose and the feel of running water. I am narrating this with the assumption that your horse is already comfortable with these elements. Once your horse has established a strong reinforcement-history with tactile work, the more challenging caretaking tasks such as sheath-cleaning will be easier to complete. However, be aware that while your horse may have been quite cooperative about the earlier tactile work, his attitude could be different when it comes to treating a new injury or cleaning the sheath.

Safety is always a consideration when working on a horse's sensitive areas. There is a substantial chance your horse could kick out at you when you get near the sheath or an injury. Be sure you're in a safe spot such as next to his belly, facing his hind end when cleaning or preparing to clean the sheath (photo 56).

Start by determining your horse's sensitivity threshold. On his belly, can you get within twelve inches of his sheath, or even perhaps as close as six inches, before he gets tense? Let's say he'll let you get to within eight inches of his sheath. Make a mental note of the location of that boundary. Then, go back another four inches so that your hand is twelve inches from the sheath. Begin making circles in that area of his abdomen. When he is complacent about your touch, bridge and reinforce. Next, make circles within ten inches of the sheath. Bridge and reinforce when he stands quietly as you touch him. Continue the process in increments of about two inches until you can touch the sheath area without much of a response from him. Bridge and reinforce his cooperation. Then, continue by touching the vulnerable areas all around the sheath including the inside of his legs.

Ultimately, you'll be able to clean inside the sheath. When you are ready to clean the penis, there may be further resistance since this is not a body part your horse is used to having touched and it is highly sensitive.

56 This is a safe spot to stand while cleaning your horse's sheath. Note that I'm facing toward his rear end, keeping an eye on his hind leg, but also staying far enough forward to avoid being kicked.

Continue to draw attention to desired behavior by bridging and reinforcing when it occurs. Progress slowly. At some point, you'll want to use a hose to help rinse, cleanse, and then re-rinse the area, since it's important to remove any soapy residue to avoid irritation. Remember, this would not be the ideal time to introduce your horse to the hose. If he is not already comfortable being sprayed with a hose for bathing, use the desensitization-procedures we discussed earlier. Choose a smooth, low-profile hose nozzle with no sharp edges. Regulate the water temperature until it's comfortably warm and hold the nozzle in your hand as you reach into the sheath to rinse thoroughly. At first, you may be able to spray water further into this area than he will allow you to reach by hand. This should complete the rinsing process, even if your horse won't allow you to fully clean the area. Eventually, he will allow you to do a thorough cleaning job in this area without resistance. As with everything else, go slowly. We have found that this process works well for us, but if you need further advice or information, consult with your veterinarian.

When deciding a regimen to follow for wound treatment, consult your veterinarian and use the same object- and tactile-desensitization process to develop your horse's trust while caring for his wound. The difference between wound treatment and sheath-cleaning is the time factor. You will most likely have enough time to go through the desensitization-process for routine sheath-cleaning, but you may not have sufficient time to complete the process in the case of caring for a wound. Wounds and injuries require immediate attention and you must do whatever is required, including sedation if your veterinarian recommends it. You can still work on tolerance in between treatments or while your horse is mildly sedated (if it is safe to feed him at that time).

You may want to teach your horse to stand with his foot in a bucket. Consider teaching this whole routine before you actually need to soak an injury. Ideally, use a broad bucket with low sides and some room for movement to help reduce the sensation of confinement. Preferably, the bucket (like some feed tubs) should be made of a soft material like rubber to prevent slipping or injury against hard sides or edges should your horse move his foot with any force. Start with the bucket on the ground where he can see it, smell it, and get comfortable with its presence. You may bridge and reinforce any of these steps. Then, ask for his foot. (There's more detail on this in the following section on farrier-behaviors.) Bridge and reinforce his compliance. Gently move his foot closer to the bucket. If he doesn't resist this move, bridge while you're moving his foot and reinforce him. Remember you are working toward the behavior you want in small steps. You are also shaping attitude in the process. Repeat the initial phase. This time, though, place his foot in the bucket. When he allows his foot to be placed in the bucket, bridge and reinforce him a few times. Then, let him stand with his foot in the bucket for just a few moments. Bridge and reinforce. Build on this procedure and then add water. The feeling of icy water, if that's what you must use, may be unpleasant, so bridge and reinforce him often. You may start with a small amount of water in the bucket and gradually add more. In the initial stages, he may kick the bucket over. Using a low-sided, rubber bucket will minimize this issue, but if it occurs, remain calm and repeat the process. You may need to break the session into smaller steps, reinforcing along the way. Set him up for success by leaving his foot in the water only a second or two at first.

Start with short sessions, then build up the time gradually, offering generous reinforcement for each successful effort. If this procedure needs to be done twice a day, soak at breakfast and dinnertimes. Then, he'll learn he eats his meal as soon as his foot is in the bucket of water. He will soon look forward to the procedure.

• *Accepting a Second Handler*

When your horse is comfortable being touched all over his body and by unusual objects, you've achieved a significant chunk of the goal I established for this section. Next, teach your horse to accept and be comfortable with a second person working on and with him.

It's important that a horse is comfortable with another person, the vet for instance, working on him. All the routine procedures the vet does, whether shots, worming, or treating an injury, involve a certain amount of unpleasantness. While it's natural for your horse to associate the vet's presence with impending discomfort, it's also easy to teach him to be stoic about, and tolerate, vet work. At Sea World, we taught the animals to cooperate with a variety of procedures. They gave urine samples and remained still for blood-drawing and X rays. Remember the killer whale we taught to keep his mouth open while his teeth were drilled?

Zoological facilities all over the world use this training system to teach their captive populations to willingly participate in both routine and extraordinary procedures. Cooperation reduces stress and injuries for both the animals and their keepers. I have seen a wide variety of target-trained animals, including elephants, hippopotamuses, rhinoceroses, hyenas, lions, tigers, and baboons to name a few. It's been my experience that horses respond to this system with the same cooperation we see in more exotic species.

When introducing a second person to further desensitize your horse, start with anyone who happens to be available and willing. Get a neighbor, a friend, or a barn-worker to help. The idea is to mimic a typical vet visit, so start by setting up the scenario. Put a halter and lead rope on your horse and hold him as you normally would for the vet. Have the second person enter the stall or come near where your horse is standing. At first, the second person should just stand quietly and not touch him or even get too close. If your horse seems relaxed, bridge and feed him. If he seems anxious, have the person simply stand near him until he relaxes, even a little. Then, bridge and feed him. The initial goal here is for your horse to focus more on you than on the second person. To help him focus, you can use the target. If he's nervous, using the target can counteract his anxiety by giving him something both constructive and familiar to do. We have stationary targets permanently mounted in our horses' stalls. During the construction of our barn, I observed a situation that really showed the significance of the target to our horses. Something fell from the hayloft, making quite a racket, and both of our horses on that side of the barn went straight to their targets and held on them. The target seemed to be a source of safety and security.

Once the horse is comfortable with a second person in his vicinity, your helper can start by getting closer to him (photo 57). Once he's relaxed with the helper near him, your helper can progress to touching the horse on the area of his body where he's most comfortable. Have your helper go through the same steps you did with your horse to achieve tactile tolerance. Your goal at the end of this process is for your horse to remain calm and relaxed while being handled by another person.

• Desensitizing for Other Procedures

Injections, worming, dental work, and the like are all part of routine horse care and are procedures your horse needs to tolerate. Start by teaching your horse to allow you to gently hold the upper and lower lips. As with the other desensitizing work we've accomplished, initiate this in small steps. Even holding his muzzle could be stressful for him. Once he accepts this, you can build up to separating his lips and massaging his gums (photo 58).

The next desensitizing process to work on is to imitate the sensation and actions involved in receiving injections and having blood drawn by doing tactile work that would feel to your horse like the work your vet does. If your vet uses an alcohol swab on the region of the neck where he administers injections and draws blood, do the same. To create a slight stinging sensation in the area, you can use a rubber band. Before you try this on your horse, try it on yourself so that you can feel what you are asking your horse to tolerate. Put the rubber band around your index finger and thumb, then pull it back slightly and let it snap against your horse's neck. Snap it very softly at first. Then bridge and reinforce a calm response to this sensation.

When your horse accepts this sensation, build from there. When he reacts calmly, reintroduce the second person and have this person help

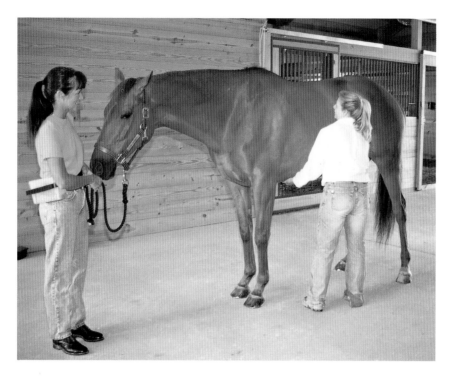

57 I'm preparing Mint for a visit from the vet. By having Darcie touch him—maybe getting close to sensitive areas, or tickling him—I can bridge and reinforce him for standing still.

58 I'm looking into George's mouth. Before I could do this, I got him used to letting me hold his muzzle with both hands (being careful not to pinch his nostrils). He fussed at first, moving his head around, but I kept holding and as soon as he settled, even for a moment, I bridged and reinforced (the clicker is in my left hand). After I could hold his muzzle, I played with his lips until he let me separate them without resistance. I rewarded him and proceeded to examine his teeth.

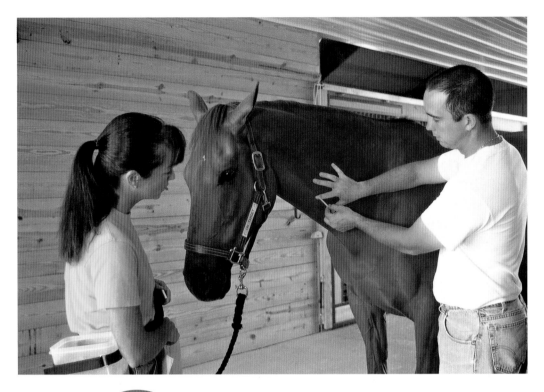

59　Vinton is holding a rubber band between his thumb and forefinger and snapping it gently against Mint's neck. This prepares Mint for an injection.

(photo 59). Once you add another person, take a few steps back to a softer sting and build back to simulating the injection. Going through this work will make injections by you or the vet a safer process.

• The Farrier

Before the farrier comes, your horse needs to be cooperative about lifting his feet. Even a very young horse can put up an amazing amount of resistance. We were once asked to work with a six-month-old miniature donkey named Milo who put up quite a fight when the farrier tried to work on him. It took four men and a tranquilizer to get the job done. We had only worked with his front feet before the farrier was scheduled to trim him and we couldn't be there for the appointment. I told the farrier we had been working with him, but I didn't tell him how much we had done with Milo. I told the farrier if things didn't go well, we would work with him the following day and set it up as a training session. The next day, the farrier said Milo was great, especially with his front feet. Milo's initial lesson with his front feet had carried over to his back feet.

Initiate foot-lifting anywhere your horse is comfortable, such as in his stall or on the cross-ties. Start by putting a little pressure on the back of his lower front leg, pushing it forward a little bit. Your horse may give to this pressure and bend his knee slightly. Bridge and reinforce the smallest release. Sometimes, though, you need to do a little more. You may need to use removal-reinforcement to set your youngster up to succeed in this instance. If so, apply some pressure to the lower tendon by pinching slightly with your thumb and finger. This will be somewhat irritating and he will probably react as if a fly landed on his leg and lift it (photos 60 and 61). Bridge and reinforce this response. Once you do this, he will begin thinking about what he did to get reinforced. Repeat the procedure, but return to the original method and apply pressure by pushing forward on the back of his lower leg. If he offers no response, repeat the application of pressure to the tendon. Your horse will soon lift his leg in response to a light touch. Then he'll start anticipating what you want when he sees you bend toward the leg and he'll lift it for you.

Once you've taught him to lift his leg, your horse needs to learn to become comfortable with his foot being held so you can clean it with a hoof pick. Next, he needs to learn to hold the foot up without leaning on you or, eventually, the farrier. Your horse may need to learn to balance himself while standing with his weight on three legs. Gradually build up the time you ask him to allow you to hold his foot and remember to bridge when he's relaxed. Feed your horse when holding his front foot (photo 62). When holding up a back foot, this isn't possible, however, this is where the bridge-signal will be very useful. With the bridge-signal, you communicate approval when he's relaxed while his hind foot is being held.

When he's mastered things at this level, begin to move his foot and leg around. Again, start with small movements and reward his lack of resistance. Then, mimic actions your farrier uses to shoe or trim your horse's feet. Stretch the front feet forward and lift his hind legs one at a time.

The first few times the farrier comes, I suggest remaining with your horse. Explain to your farrier the way you are training him. Then, bridge and reinforce your horse for good behavior. Stand near him and draw his

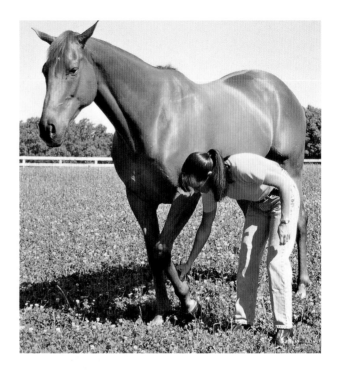

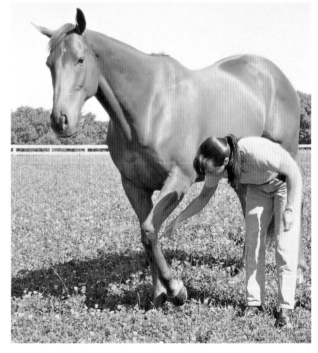

60-61 I'm teaching Mint to lift his leg in these pictures. First I pinch the back of his leg and he lifts it. I bridge and reinforce. Eventually, all I have to do is bend down and point at his leg for him to lift it. He does this to avoid your pinching him (removal-reinforcement) as well as get his treat (reward-reinforcement).

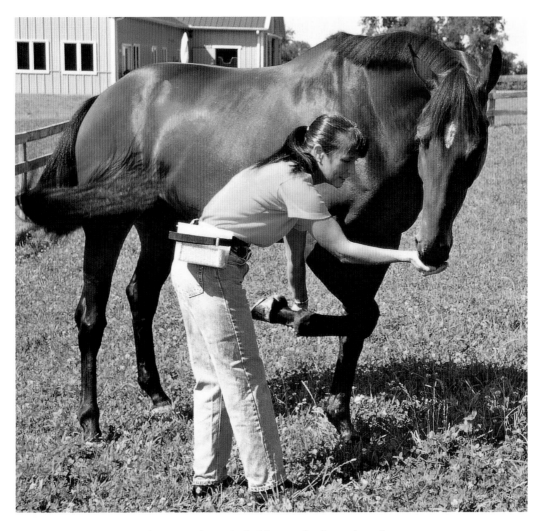

62 You can reinforce your horse for holding up his leg without leaning on you as I'm doing here with George.

attention to desired behavior. However, be aware of what the farrier is doing so your efforts are not disrupting his work. Most likely the farrier will be pleased you're trying to make the job easier.

LOADING AND SHIPPING

There are few tasks more stressful, frustrating, and potentially dangerous than loading an unwilling, frightened horse into a trailer. Many horses are reluctant loaders. Vinton and I are frequently questioned about this common problem. The list of reasons why horses don't want to load is probably endless. It could be the confinement of the trailer or the isolation from other horses. Some horses may not like the movement of the trailer or being unloaded at a strange place such as the veterinary hospital, a different barn, or a horse show. Horses are quick studies in trailering situations. They easily figure out how to avoid the things they don't like doing, just as they are quick to determine how to get the things they do want. Whether your horse is new at trailer loading or an unwilling veteran, take the time to build up a strong reinforcement-history associated with trailering. Teach him that good things happen when he's in or around the trailer.

A horse with no experience in the trailer should progress much faster than a reluctant veteran. Our horses easily learned to load at an early age. When Mint was three and George was a yearling, they learned to load themselves into the trailer in two sessions over the course of a day. We did one session with them in the morning and the second session at lunchtime. At dinnertime, we had planned to work with them individually on other behaviors. However, the trailer was still in the indoor arena and they each walked into the ring and loaded themselves without being asked. You can teach your horse, no matter what his attitude is toward loading, to do the same. All you need is a little time, patience, and, of course, reinforcement.

Teach your horse the fundamentals of trailering once you have established his On Target Training foundation. He should recognize the bridge-signal and be adept at target-training with both a hand-held and stationary target. If possible, park the trailer in an area where you can work while your horse is loose, without a halter and lead rope. An enclosed ring, indoors or out, is ideal, but you can accomplish the same goal anywhere adding a halter and lead rope. Horses seem to gain confidence faster when they are loose, but you may not be in the position to train that way. You may need to work on loading in a parking lot, for example, which will require use of a halter and lead line. It's fine to use a halter and lead rope when you have to, as long as you use the equipment to contain, rather than coerce, your horse. Be sure to allow your horse room to move. We want him to *choose* to be near the trailer.

Since most people have a two-horse trailer, I've chosen to give instructions in this text for loading into one. However, the photos in the chapter illustrate loading into a four-horse trailer for those of you who use one of these. First, open the divider between the stalls before you start to allow plenty of room. Begin by allowing your horse to become comfortable with the presence of the trailer. Let him see and smell it. Walk all around it so he can investigate the outside, the front, the sides, and the ramp. Walk with him, using the target to get him close. Place the target near the side of the trailer. When he touches it, bridge and reinforce. If your horse has an unpleasant association with the trailer, or if he's simply afraid, you may need to bridge and reinforce when he gets within ten feet of it or wherever is comfortable for him. Approach from the side instead of the back; this different angle will most likely allow you to get closer with a nervous horse (photos 63 and 64). Walk all around it at first, doing circles and figure-eights. Walk past the ramp and then make circles near the ramp, utilizing the target. Walk circles at the sides of the trailer, and gradually shift your circle over until you are walking your horse directly toward the trailer ramp. Always bridge and reinforce as you go toward the trailer, feeding while he's closest to the trailer. Utilizing circles and figure-eights can help your horse focus on what he is doing, not where he is doing it, which will allow you to gradually shift closer to the trailer ramp without him becoming defensive.

If your horse resists, make a mental note of how close he can comfortably get before he begins to balk. This becomes the threshold for progress. Don't try to force your horse forward. This will only increase his apprehension. Instead, hold the target in front of him, perhaps a foot in front of his nose. Most likely, he will stretch his neck out to touch the target without moving his feet forward. Nevertheless, bridge and reinforce, but offer the feed where the target was. Then circle and walk away from the trailer. Do not feed while walking away. Leaving an uncomfortable situation is sufficient reinforcement. As your circle takes you back toward the trailer, bridge and reinforce while he is taking steps toward the trailer. This is the action we want to see repeated. At this point, he may not be any closer to the trailer but he is moving in the right direction.

Next, walk up to your threshold area. Ask your horse to target just before that spot where he became nervous before, and then bridge and reinforce his correct response. Afterward, hold the target about a foot past the threshold point, closer to the trailer. Bridge and reinforce, offering food where you held the target. Most likely, your horse will take a step forward to eat more comfortably and, in the process, get closer to the trailer. By now, the whole scenario should be positive and non-threatening.

63-64 Before trying to load your horse into the trailer itself, walk around it as I'm doing here with Mint. This gets him used to all the aspects of the trailer. (Note, he's following me without a halter or lead rope and without my using a target). Let him look at the trailer ramp, too.

The act of eating actually brings about a relaxation response in horses, which further enhances the experience. You are more relaxed too, because you are not struggling with your horse to go toward the trailer.

Continue in this way until your horse easily approaches the trailer. The length of time he takes to willingly approach the trailer will, of course, vary with each horse. You may need to make the steps smaller and more reinforcing. You may be able to progress quite quickly. Monitor your horse's reaction as you get nearer to gauge his progress and determine when to take the next step. He should be relaxed at each step before you move closer. Keep the sessions brief.

Your horse will make it clear when he is not overly concerned about the presence of the trailer. At that point, he will probably be eager to get close to the trailer because he will have the chance to be reinforced. Next, go through the same steps toward the ramp or step-up. Ask him to follow the target and take steps forward until he has one foot on the ramp or has taken a step up if you are using a step-up or stock trailer. When he takes that step, bridge and reinforce him. If you are working with him while he's wearing a halter and lead rope, provide enough slack in the rope so he can back up. Don't reinforce him with food for backing out, but allow him the freedom to escape if he feels he needs to at this point to help minimize his fear. If he feels trapped, he may panic in a more dramatic way and could rear or spin around. Draw attention to the desired behavior. If you have taken your time with this, you are unlikely to see your horse panic at all. Continue taking small steps into the trailer. Allow your horse to back out if he chooses. He'll soon realize that all the food-reinforcement is given when he is in, or going toward, the trailer. Occasionally, walk him away from the trailer and at your initiative (not his), back him out.

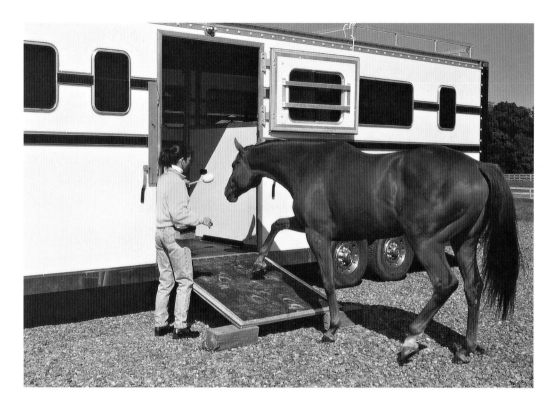

65-67 I'm loading Mint into a five-horse trailer using the target. I'm pleased to see him lifting his right leg up and on to the ramp, so I bridge and reinforce. I then move into the trailer myself and reward him when he brings his other front leg up. He follows me all the way in where I reward him again.

This would be a good time to incorporate the stationary target into the session. Mount the stationary target in front of the chest bar where your horse can see it while loading and where he can also touch it. This will also position him where you want him so you can close the back doors. As he grows more comfortable walking further onto the trailer, point out the stationary target and ask him to target. When you first do this, you will probably need to be inside the trailer to point the target out to him. After he targets this way, build up the time he holds on it. Next, send him to the target by pointing to it from the back of the trailer. When he loads himself and touches the target, bridge and reinforce and again build up the time he holds on the target. Teach him to hold on the target long enough for you to go around to the front door or hatch and reinforce him. Next, extend the time he holds on the target even more.

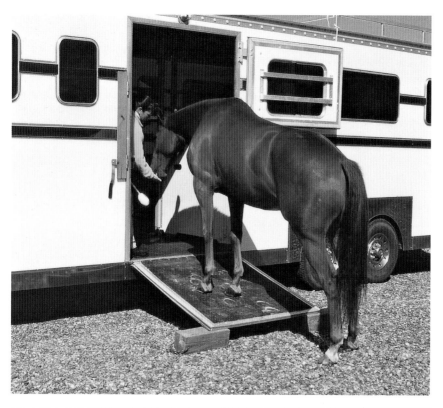

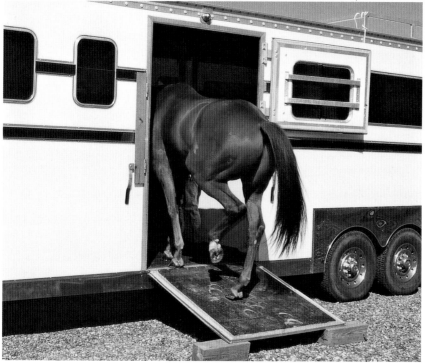

It would be helpful to line up an assistant for the following part of the training. If not, you can work alone, if in an enclosed area. The next goal is to attach the butt bar and close the ramp, but first you need to desensitize your horse to the sounds, movements, and sensations that he'll experience when the trailer is being closed. If you are working alone, continue to reinforce at the trailer door. If you have a helper, situate one person at the front of the trailer and the other at the back. When your horse walks into the trailer, continue to leave his head untied. Have your assistant begin to rattle the moveable trailer parts such as the hooks and chains. When you start, your assistant should keep himself off to the side in case the horse kicks out or suddenly backs off the trailer. We are building trust so allow him to back off if he wishes. Soon, he will ignore the commotion and won't have the desire to leave. As you start the process and he stands quietly, bridge and reinforce him. When you bridge, he may back out. Wait for him to walk back on before feeding him. He'll quickly realize he only gets fed in the front, so he'll begin to wait there for reinforcement.

Proceed to move the butt bar and rub it against his hindquarters. Even though he may be fine with this sort of tactile work in his stall, his senses are heightened on the trailer. Take small steps. When you can hook and unhook the butt bar without reaction from him, build up his time in the trailer. When the butt bar is first attached, he may test it. If he does, ask him to target. When he targets in a relaxed manner, bridge and reinforce, then detach the butt bar. You don't want him to think that anxious behavior will get the butt bar undone faster. Instead, you want him to think that the bar will be detached faster when he settles down. Once your horse is comfortable with the butt bar being opened and closed, you can progress to attaching the trailer-tie to his halter. Before unhooking the butt bar, be sure to unhook the trailer-tie from his halter and then ask him to back out. If you have a stock trailer without a ramp, teaching your horse to back off will take some confidence building. Some horses worry about backing off the ramp, too. In either circumstance, you should reinforce backing out when asked nearly as much as you reinforce walking into the trailer. Then, ask him to step back into the trailer. When he commits, bridge and reinforce.

Backing out of the trailer is a matter of both trust and confidence. What can you do to help set him up to succeed? Start by really solidifying backing-up on the ground. He should have a distinct back-up cue that he responds to readily. Next, park the trailer in a way that minimizes the step down or the angle of the trailer ramp, perhaps with the trailer's rear

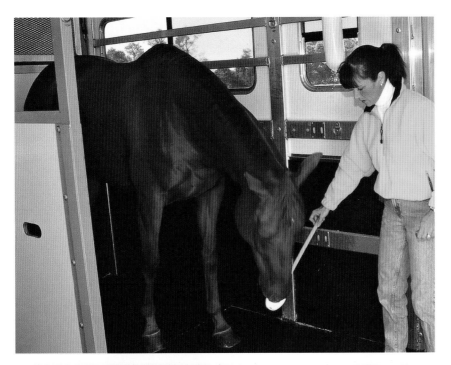

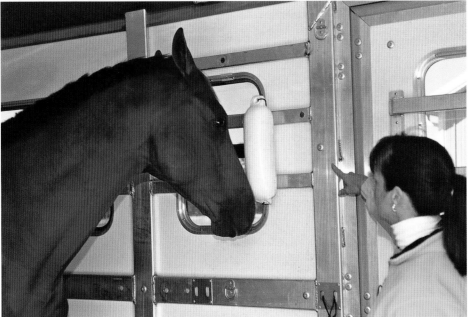

68-69 In these photos I'm encourage Mint to back into the five-horse-trailer stall by using the target. I lower the target back, under his nose, so when he follows it, he will back-up. Once in there, I ask him to hold on the stationary target that is already in place. As soon as he is settled, I bridge and reinforce.

tires against a curb or incline. This is a good intermediate step. Use the target as an aid. The target can serve as a focal point for your horse and will help regulate his backward pace. Another step might be to get his two front feet on the ramp and then use the target to ask him to back out. This is another way to help build his confidence with the ramp while his back feet are on even ground. Next, get your horse a little further into the trailer and back him off until he is going all the way in, and backing all the way off, in a calm manner.

If you've been working with two people, it's time to start fading-out the person at the front of the trailer. The person in the back will take over bridging and reinforcing. When the person in front of the trailer was doing the bridging and reinforcing, the horse's focus was on her, not on the activity behind him. With this change, the horse learns to hold on the target and ignore the second person. His focus will switch to the one person who remains. To fade-out the person at the front, have her stand a few feet from the door while your horse loads. Each time he loads, have the second person step back further until the horse is no longer concerned with her presence.

If your schedule allows, take advantage of mealtimes. Ask your horse to load in the trailer. Close the trailer and feed him his meals in there for the next few days. As soon as he finishes his food, open up the trailer and take him off. As your horse gets comfortable with the process, reinforce him for exiting the trailer. This is also a behavior we shouldn't take for granted.

I concentrated on loading into to a two-horse trailer since it's the type many people use, but you can apply these loading lessons to any type of trailer or van.

Once your horse is comfortable loading and standing inside the trailer, it's time to start preparing him for shipping. Standing and balancing on a moving trailer are not easy tasks when you don't have hands to help steady you or know which way you'll move. Julie Winkel, Vinton's first instructor, succinctly illustrated this point for her students. She had them stand in the horse trailer holding two buckets of water as she drove around the farm! It's very important to make the trailer ride as smooth as possible. Avoid sudden stops, sharp turns, fast take-offs, and bumps and potholes when possible. These are easy steps to bypass shipping trauma. Traveling a long distance is tiring for horses. Remember to stop every few hours to check hay and water and give them a brief rest. Also, be sure there is fresh air flowing through the trailer.

70-71 Some horses tend to rush out of the trailer, which is potentially extremely dangerous, so it's important to have them walk out calmly as Mint is doing in these photos. I taught him to walk out quietly by stopping him on the ramp using the target, rewarding, then continuing on another step or two before stopping again and rewarding. Now he unloads (and loads) without the target or reward.

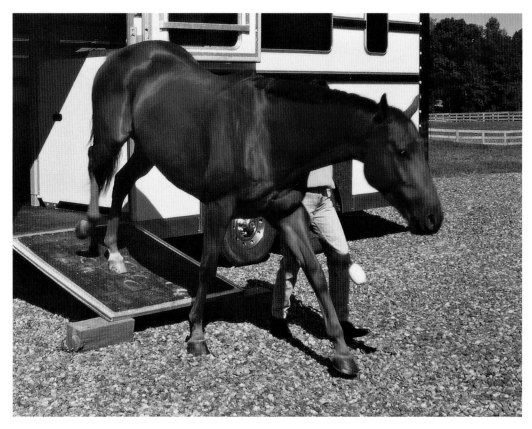

As you begin introducing your horse to shipping with brief trips, get a helper if you can. Then one person can drive and the other can bridge and reinforce the horse while the trailer is moving. The first "trip" should be about fifty feet, just long enough to let your horse experience movement. Bridge and reinforce his calm behavior. If you bridge while the trailer is moving and he gets too distracted to eat, wait this out. Reinforce once he relaxes even slightly. If necessary, use the target to help him focus. Then take him off the trailer and end the session. On the next day, repeat the process while driving about two hundred feet. The third day, gradually build up the length of the trip, keeping in mind that it may be illegal for a person to travel inside the trailer on public roads. Once your horse is relaxed about these short trips that end right where he started, begin short trips that end somewhere a bit different, such as another area of the farm.

When your horse loads and ships short distances without getting anxious, take the next trip without the person in the trailer. Load your horse, reinforce well, hang a hay net, and close up the trailer. Having hay on the trailer allows him to be reinforced as you travel. You may also take another horse with you; however, be sure that the horses get along. Don't let a social problem become an issue while you're teaching your horse to trailer calmly. After all, you want to set him up to succeed at this venture.

Through this training, your horse will soon be an experienced shipper. If you don't regularly ship him, take him on practice trips from time to time. When an emergency arises, your horse's shipping lessons will be fresh for him and getting on and off the trailer will be an easy, familiar routine.

Saddle Wise

INTRODUCING TACK

Our next focus will be on the performance-oriented tasks that allow us to prepare for what we want to do with our horses under saddle. Your horse may be green or he may be a veteran with some rough spots or behavior problems. For either situation, the approach will be the same. Step-by-step, you'll be balancing his reinforcement-history through the training process. Let's start with the most fundamental step for good under-saddle work, accepting tack for the first time. Your horse needs to become familiar and comfortable with each piece of equipment you plan to use. He should be nonchalant about seeing you carrying the saddle near him, and the act of lifting it over your head should not spook him.

Start introducing tack in an area where he is comfortable. Be sure he is able to see the equipment clearly. Bridge and reinforce your horse's calm, accepting responses as you introduce the equipment, using the desensitization principles outlined in Chapter Four. Once your horse tolerates the tack, you can get started. Put your horse's halter on and attach the lead rope. Begin by taking a small step back and repeat one of the steps you used in the desensitization process. Perhaps rub him with the saddle pad. Then progress to placing the saddle pad on his back. Bridge and reinforce him for standing still. If it takes a moment for him to settle, that's fine. If he shows a less accepting response, step back to the desensitization procedure. If he's gone through all the earlier training steps, the saddle pad and other tack should not concern him. When he's relaxed about the pad on his back, ask him to walk a step or two, then bridge and reinforce a calm response.

Next, progress to the saddle. Before placing it on your horse's back, remove the fittings and accessories so there is nothing for him to cope with except the weight of the saddle. First, hold the saddle over his back. If he stands quietly, bridge and reinforce him. Then, gently place the saddle on his back. If he stands quietly when you do this, bridge and reinforce him immediately. In fact, feed him a few handfuls as he gets used to the weight and feel of the saddle. If he seems nervous, bridge and reinforce each little step toward relaxation. When he seems calm, feed him a few handfuls and carefully remove the saddle. Then, bridge and reinforce him for allowing you to remove the saddle. Standing quietly when the saddle is removed is a desirable behavior and worth reinforcing, but be aware that you want him to get more reinforcement when the saddle is on his back.

Repeat the process a few times over the next day or so. When your horse is comfortable wearing the saddle, ask him to take a few steps with it on his back. Even under this small amount of extra weight, his balance will be a bit different and he may need time to adjust. Continue to draw attention to desired behavior as he gets comfortable. Remember to keep the sessions short and pleasant.

When your horse is comfortable wearing a saddle, it's time to add the girth or cinch. Be sure to introduce him to one that is loose enough to allow him to adjust to the feel of it before it's tightened. This piece of tack touches the horse in a sensitive, vulnerable area. Allow your horse some time to get used to it.

Put the saddle pad and saddle on the horse's back. Bridge and reinforce him. Next, attach the girth to the saddle. Bridge and reinforce his acceptance of this addition to his equipment. Move to the other side of your horse. When you reach under him to grab the girth, be aware that this movement might startle your horse, so go slowly. If he stands quietly, bridge and reinforce. Now, allow the girth to lightly touch the girth area. Bridge and reinforce him while holding the girth against him (photos 72 and 73). If he starts getting anxious, softly tell him "whoa," and remain calm and steady. Horses are sensitive to our reactions, so keep yours positive.

Look for the slightest improvement in relaxation, then bridge and reinforce this. Repeat the process until your horse is relaxed with this

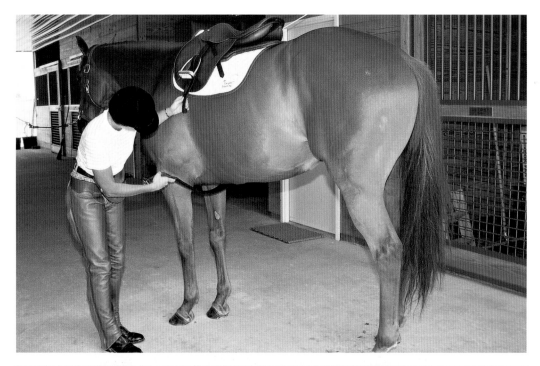

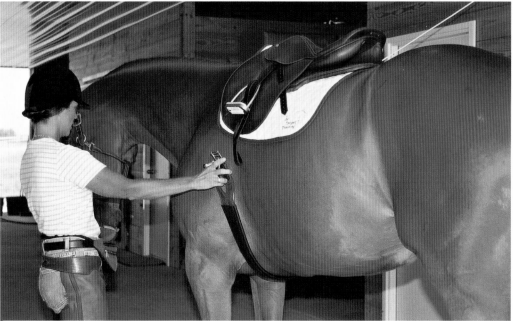

72-73 When you first train your horse to the saddle (or retrain a "girthy" animal) bring the girth under him and as it touches his belly use a verbal bridge-signal ("ok," or "good boy," or whatever you choose) and reward with food in your left hand.

action. Next, fasten the girth so it barely makes contact. Bridge and reinforce his quiet reaction. If this goes well, tighten the girth a short increment. Then, walk him a step or two forward, bridge and reinforce. Do several sessions like this over the next few days. In each session, walk a bit more and tighten the girth a bit more. Since there is no weight being put in the saddle, there is no need at first to fully tighten it. Sometimes, horses learn to hold their breath when being girthed. Going slowly now will help to prevent this protective response from developing later.

If your horse is experienced and has a persistent problem with girthing, follow the same process. First, determine if an ill-fitting saddle or a physical difficulty is at the root of his behavior problem. If you do find a physical cause and correct it, your horse may still associate the saddle with his previous discomfort and anticipate pain when it is placed on his back. You will need to build a new reinforcement-history for saddling, so go through the preceding steps, and rebuild his association using reward-reinforcement. The training process may take longer for your horse than for an inexperienced horse learning these lessons for the first time. Remember that he is acting difficult during saddling because it has worked for him in the past. Ignore his problematic behavior as much as possible and continue the training. He will learn that his actions won't prevent the girth from being tightened. When his fussing diminishes, offer him reward- and removal-reinforcement (easing of the pressure of the girth). A target might help at this stage. To give him something besides the feeling of the girth to concentrate on, have him hold on a stationary target or have an assistant use a hand-held target. Remember to take your time.

Follow the same method for adding a bridle to your horse's equipment. The type of bridle you use, as well as the type of bit, if any, will depend on your horse and your training program. As I take you through the bridling process and through the upcoming training scenarios, keep in mind that these are examples of how we incorporate On Target Training into our training program. On Target Training can be added to any program and be adapted to your training method.

First of all, review the methods I used when I first put on a halter since most bridling is the same. The difference is the addition of the bit. Usually, you'll need to encourage him to open his mouth—at least for the first few times. Do this by inserting your fingers in his mouth where the bit will rest. Start with a mild snaffle bit that you would use for a sensitive horse, nothing severe or harsh. Use your fingers to help guide the bit into his mouth.

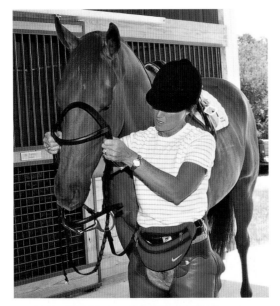

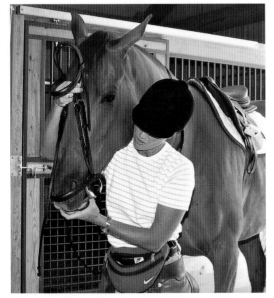

Try to avoid letting the bit hit any of his teeth. Have you ever hit one of your teeth by accident with a spoon? Put on the bridle before feeding breakfast and dinner, the first few days, to build a strong, affirmative association with wearing it. I recommend first checking for wolf teeth or other dental issues like sharp hooks that would make eating with a bit painful. Keep an eye on him the first meal to be sure this builds a positive association with the bridge and bit. Remove the bridle, avoiding hitting his teeth, when he's finished his meal. If you use On Target Training from the beginning, your horse will most likely be very responsive. When he is comfortable wearing the bridle and eating with the bit in, begin to lead him in the bridle with the reins attached to get him used to the pressure and the feeling of being led by the reins. In addition to bridging and reinforcing correct responses, be sure to appropriately soften or release any pressure.

74-76 I'm starting to bridle Mint in a manner familiar to most of you, but notice that once he has accepted the bit calmly, I bridge and reward him immediately with some food even before I finish bringing the headstall over his ears and attaching the throatlatch and noseband.

LONGE-LINE LESSONS

At this stage, your horse has a very strong foundation. You have probably noticed that he's learning faster all the time. The lessons he's learned will make his transition to a performance horse pleasant for him and you. There are many different methods for preparing a horse for under-saddle work. Our On Target Training system is effective both alone or with any other program we have come across.

First, we'll focus on longeing, which is one of the traditional methods used to train horses for hundreds of years and is an excellent way to prepare a young horse for under-saddle work. The difference in our approach to this classic method is the addition of the On Target Training system to increase motivation and improve communication. Remember that the scenario I describe is offered as an example of adding On Target Training to one method of longeing. If you rely on another technique, you can continue to do it as you are most comfortable and just factor in On Target Training. I am not an expert on longeing but there are many books and other resources available to learn more.

Before we get started, I'd like to share an anecdote that illustrates how the addition of our system to classic horse training can make the lessons you're teaching clearer and more motivating for your horse. I continually try to learn as much as possible about horses and how they're trained. Some time ago, when I had just begun working with horses, I took the opportunity to watch someone teach a young horse to longe. This young mare had already had some initial training and was beginning to understand what was expected of her. She was one of those horses who would rather do anything but stand still. As a result, she had trouble halting when she was asked to stop on the longe line. The trainer tried to correct her, which only got her more excited. Finally, the mare stopped and stood perfectly still. Can you guess what happened then? Nothing. The mare's reward was to be left alone. She wasn't corrected any further, meaning that the aversive was removed. This is the way traditional horse training goes. I was so accustomed in my training work to drawing attention to good behavior that I could barely contain myself as I watched. I'm convinced that it's far more effective to have both reward- and removal-reinforcement tools at our disposal when we train. In some situations we correct undesired behavior, but it's also important to regularly draw attention to and reward good behavior.

When training a horse to longe, we combine reward- and removal-reinforcement to create a highly effective teaching and learning experience. Our horses start their longe work wearing a halter, but you can certainly use a longeing cavesson or any other equipment you prefer. We use a longe line and a longe whip. You can also use the target as a longeing aid. Set the target on a longer pole than you use for other purposes—about twelve feet is a useful length. Using a target in this manner allows your horse to be motivated to go forward through reward-reinforcement instead of being motivated with the whip from behind, which is removal-reinforcement. In fact, you could get him to go forward on the line solely through reward-reinforcement by teaching him to follow the target in all three gaits (photos 77–80). Once he masters the concept, fade-out the target.

I'm going to illustrate, however, how to integrate our On Target Training system with a traditional longeing method. Again, no matter how you usually teach a horse in these early lessons, you can enhance his learning experience by combining your methods with our system.

First, attach the longe line to one side of the halter, depending on which side you want to begin. Most likely, your horse will be more comfortable starting on the left if you taught him to lead in that direction. The longe line should be short in the beginning to allow you more control of your horse. Decide which cues you want to use to teach your horse each gait. We use the words walk, trot, canter, whoa, back-up, and a cluck as a cue to move forward or go faster. Even though your horse won't understand the cues at this early stage, use them anyway. Before you know it, he'll be responding to them.

Be sure your horse is desensitized to all the longeing equipment, including the whip. You'll use the whip as an aversive to motivate him to go forward, but he shouldn't fear the whip. Instead, teach him to respect its movement.

Hold the longe line in your leading hand and the longe whip in the other hand. Take a step back, facing the horse. If your horse stands still, bridge and reinforce. Waiting for a cue on what to do next is a desirable behavior and shouldn't be taken for granted. Step back again. The hand holding the longe line should be aligned with your horse's shoulder. The whip should be held straight out from your body to the side so the lash points toward the horse's hindquarters.

As you say "walk," begin moving on the axis of a circle. The horse shouldn't pull you off your small circle. Maintain boundaries. As you

77-80 In the first two pictures I'm teaching George to longe using a longer version of a target to motivate him to go forward rather than using the traditional longe whip. I still use the longe line in the normal way, but in the second two pictures I have dispensed with it to give him more freedom since I'm confident he will just follow the target. Because he is no longer on the longe line, I can ask him to come to me each time I bridge and reward him for a correct response. (The whole

exercise would have been easier for him if the pole had been longer since he could
have made a larger circle around me. If possible adapt the types of poles used to clean
a swimming pool since they are quite long.)

81-83   When I longe in the traditional manner with a line
and whip, I combine removal- and reward-
reinforcement. I "remove" (deactivate) the
use of the whip as soon as my horse responds
to my voice and body cues correctly. I reinforce him for making the correct choices by
bridging him as I stand in the center expecting him to wait for his reward until I walk up
to him out on the circle.

begin pivoting on the circle, your shoulders will move which brings the
whip to your horse's side (where your leg will eventually be) to form more
of a triangle with your body and the horse's position. If you need to
encourage forward movement, move the whip toward your horse. Start
with small movements. You don't want to panic him. You just want him
to walk forward. At this stage, your horse is still fairly close to you so you
can touch his hindquarters with the whip, if necessary. As soon as he
moves forward, bridge and reinforce. You are teaching him a concept in
this lesson and want him to think it through. Step back again. Bridge and
reinforce him on an occasional basis for standing still until given a cue.

    An advantage of being in close proximity to your horse at this stage is
you can use the longe line like a lead rope, which gives you more control
if necessary. As your horse begins to understand the lesson, move further
away from him and increase the circumference of the longeing circle. If
he doesn't stand quietly before you cue him, squarely face him and pull
on the longe line as you did with the lead rope. Say "whoa," gently snap
the longe line in an up-down motion, and repeat until he stops. The verbal cue "whoa," the squared body position, and the snapping of the longe
line all serve to communicate the desired response to your horse. (Soon

you should not need to snap the longe line. Eventually, he will understand the verbal cue and your body position.) In this instance, you're using removal-reinforcement. The movement against the halter feels annoying to horses. When he stands still, reward him by bridging and reinforcing. You don't have to feed every time. When you bridge correct behavior, you draw attention to it. The longe-line behavior we want to emphasize most now is stopping and standing, so continue to bridge and reinforce your horse for doing this.

Continue the longe-line lesson by stepping back again and saying, "walk." Circle with your horse, keeping the whip in proximity to his hindquarters. You'll need to use the whip less frequently as your horse gets reinforced for moving forward. If he doesn't respond to the cue to walk, keep the longe whip directly behind him. This way, you pair the whip behind him with the cue to walk, which gives the command significance. Soon, he will listen to the verbal cue and the longe whip can be held toward the horse's side. When you want him to go, you should be able to face in the direction the horse moves as you pivot on the circle. He will learn that when you face him, that means he is to stop. As you face forward again and raise your arm toward his side, he should move forward. Your verbal cue will tell him the pace to maintain. Have him walk on the longe in both directions, and keep these initial sessions short and easy. Try to end each lesson on a good note when your horse is relaxed. At this early point, you're trying to exercise your horse's mind on the longe line instead of physically working him. You want him to look forward to the next sessions.

If your horse has difficulty with these exercises, take a step back to leading, using the longe line as a lead rope. Bridge and reinforce correct behavior and then slowly return to the longeing position. When your horse walks and stops on cue in both directions, expand your circle. To prepare to teach trotting and cantering, decrease the circumference of your circle again to increase control.

Begin working on trotting using the same steps you did at the walk. Work on the walk and whoa cues as well. When your horse is adept at discriminating between these three cues he's learned, increase the size of the circle in small increments. When he is going well and following the cues for walk, whoa, and trot on a twenty-meter circle, you can begin teaching him to canter on the longe line.

Some people think it's difficult to teach the canter depart on the longe, but it shouldn't be at this stage of On Target Training. Your horse is completely familiar with reward-reinforcement and he has a vested interest in figuring out what you are asking. You have already established longeing at the walk and trot, and he understands the meaning of the whip, the "cluck," and the word "whoa." Strive for the canter by starting out with your horse moving well forward on the circumference of your chosen circle. When you want him to pick up the canter, encourage him forward with the whip, a strong "cluck," and say the word "canter." As soon as he strikes off in the canter, bridge. Before long he will understand the word "canter" through bridging and rewarding the correct gait. Once he clearly comprehends the canter-depart cue, begin to refine the canter by rewarding relaxation and a steady, rhythmical gait.

Once you have established the trot and canter on the longe line, focus on tempo. During trot work, condition your horse to a "cluck" sound by clucking and following it with a wave of the whip. Soon, he'll respond to the sound alone.

One of the purposes of the longe-line lessons is to teach your horse to respond to these verbal cues before getting on his back. It's much safer and less confusing for him to learn without a rider. Next, accustom him to wearing tack on the longe line, but take several steps back to the beginning work and keep everything short, sweet, and very clear. To avoid straining his legs, don't keep him on a small circle for an extended time period.

Start by putting on the saddle minus fittings or anything that could flap. Since your horse has previously accepted wearing a saddle and walking with it on his back, you can safely add the experience of longeing under saddle. You might have him walk on the longe line the first day and then add trot work the second day. Even if you haven't got a reaction to the saddle yet, you might get one when you ask him to trot. Keep him moving forward and keep yourself on your circle. Bridge and reinforce trot work on the line only when he is settled, not bucking or playing. When your horse can walk, trot, canter, and stop on the longe line in both directions, add the saddle fittings. Reduce the circle size to gain more control and increase it when he shows you he knows what is expected.

The bridle is the next addition. Remove the reins and put the bridle on under the halter, with the longe line attached to the halter. When he is very responsive at all three gaits as well as stopping and standing, you can try the next step. He must be solid in his training up to this point and comfortable with bit pressure before you attempt this. We suggest you run the longe line through the inner bit ring, up over your horse's poll, and snap it to the opposite bit ring. This allows for even pressure on both sides and prevents the bit from being pulled through the mouth. Go through the same steps and when he gets accustomed to this, put the reins on the bridle and secure them. When your horse can calmly and consistently longe in both directions wearing tack, you can prepare for mounting.

INTRODUCING THE RIDER

As you prepare your horse to accept being mounted, try to put yourself in his place. Consider what he will encounter that could be new and unusual and how you might teach him to be at ease as he learns. Initially, he will need to accustom himself to the change in position and proximity of his handler and soon-to-be rider. The next and most significant change will come when he must first adjust to weight in the stirrup and then adapt to that weight shifting over and on to his back. Once he gets somewhat comfortable with these dramatic changes, he will have to learn to balance himself under the weight of a rider at all gaits. The balancing process is likely to be awkward for him and is, therefore, potentially unsettling.

To make this major transition a smooth one, start with some desensitization work. Tack your horse as you usually do but put a halter and lead rope over his bridle. If he's a bit nervous, do a longeing session before you begin this desensitization session to help him focus his mind on working. You may want to begin by having a helper hold your horse, but if he seems fairly nonchalant, you could try the following introductory steps yourself.

Begin by allowing your horse to sniff and examine the stool or portable-mounting block you'll be using to mount. I suggest using a portable block that you can take to him or easily reposition. Once he seems relaxed about this new object, set it down to his left in the place where you would use it to mount. When he stands still, bridge and reinforce. Take a step up. If he accepts this calmly, take the second step up if necessary. Bridge and reinforce from that position. If at first he moves around to face you to eat, that's not a big concern. Reposition the block and step up again. If he remains where he is and doesn't swing around toward you, bridge and reinforce him again immediately to emphasize the idea that he will get fed when you and the block are in a specific proximity from him. Once he understands this concept and stands quietly when you step on to the block or stool, you can repeat this procedure at a permanent mounting block or other location to help him apply his new knowledge to multiple situations.

When your horse is comfortable standing for you at any mounting block, it's time to prepare him for the sensations of movement and shifting weight in the saddle. Pat the saddle and apply some weight on his back with your hands. Remember to proceed slowly in small steps. Bridge and reinforce correct responses. As your horse gets accustomed to these new sensations, increase the weight on the saddle and his back as well as movement in the saddle area. Put the heel of your palm in the stirrup and push down slightly. Increase the pressure as he becomes more comfortable. To mimic the weight shifts he'll feel as you mount, grab the pommel and cantle and move the saddle side to side. Next, move to the mounting block and repeat the steps. Be certain your horse is comfortable with each stage before you proceed further. If he regresses, take steps back and build up his confidence. If he is not successfully adapting in these sessions, he has not been reinforced enough and you have most likely moved ahead too quickly. Each horse is different and some will progress faster than others. Be flexible in your expectations.

The next step, once your horse is comfortable with the preceding one, is to accustom him to the sensation of your foot in the stirrup. During this experience, a helper can be a valuable asset. Before you introduce this step, you may want to longe your horse to get him focused and provide an opportunity for him to expend some energy. As you longe him, gauge his level of compliance. If your horse is not having a focused day on the longe line, it's probably not the best day to begin this work. Remember, by going more slowly, you actually speed your progress in the long run and avoid potential problems.

If the work on the longe line goes well, desensitize your horse to movement in the saddle while another person holds him. That person should be the one to bridge and reinforce him. In addition to working on the mounting block to increase the horse's tolerance toward accepting a rider, desensitize him on the ground. Stand at mounting position on the ground and place a hand on the saddle while lightly jumping up and down. When your horse ignores this activity, have your assistant bridge and reinforce. Next, increase the movement and weight on the saddle. When your horse accepts this stage, have your helper lead him at the walk while you lean on the saddle. As he's led, the assistant should bridge and reinforce correct responses. Your horse is probably ready to accept the weight of a rider when he is at ease.

84-85 When I mount a horse for the first time, I prepare him for my weight by dragging and leaning on the stirrup, and tugging on the saddle. At the same time, my assistant Tammy is bridging and reinforcing him if he is quiet.

Next, add more weight and place your arms and shoulders across the saddle while maintaining a position that will allow you to hop off immediately should the need arise (photos 84–88). Progress to walking in this manner as the person leading bridges and reinforces correct behavior. When this stage has been accepted, it's time to sit astride the horse by quietly swinging your leg over the saddle. Keep the movement of your leg deliberate. You don't want to inadvertently startle your horse by brushing your leg over his hindquarters. That step can come once he comfortably accepts a rider on his back. Your horse may also find it startling to glimpse the rider on his back from the corner of his eye. To avoid this problem, keep your head and shoulders low when you first get on and gradually sit up straighter as your horse accepts your presence on his back. Bridge and reinforce this process.

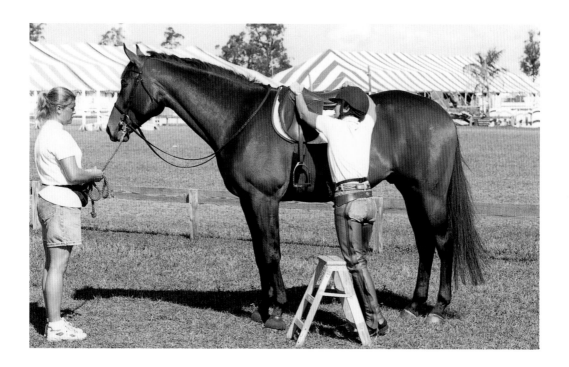

If your horse is experienced and has a problem with mounting, follow the previous steps once you determine there is no physical reason for the difficulty. If you can isolate the point in mounting where the problem arises, pay special attention to that step, making it as reinforcing as possible. For example, let's say your horse scoots away from the mounting block. Spend more time with this phase, but still work the other steps so the whole process is reinforcing for him. Consider what you can do to set him up to succeed. If your horse tends to walk away when you're halfway in the saddle, you may want to initiate mounting facing him in a corner of the paddock or arena so it's not as easy to walk away.

If he bolts or becomes overly excited during the mounting process, the help of an assistant as a ground person would be useful. This person can hold a target and bridge and reinforce the horse for holding on the target as you mount. Reinforce correct actions with three or four handfuls of feed so the horse learns to stand and wait in anticipation of more reinforcement coming. The ground person can ask the horse to take a step or two following the target. Bridge and reinforce walking, stopping, and

86-88   Then, I mount and stay forward and low so I don't spook him—many horses are disturbed by the sight of something high above them. When he seems comfortable, I slowly sit up and Tammy leads us forward while bridging and reinforcing him if he remains calm.

touching the target. The target helps take the focus away from the rider as you rebuild his reinforcement-history and provides opportunities to reinforce correct mounting behavior. When your horse is ready, switch the focus from the ground person to the rider by having the rider bridge and reinforce while the ground person holds the target. Then fade-out the ground person. Your horse will now have more motivation to stand still during the mounting. I recommend varying how much you feed at this stage. Sometimes feed one handful, sometimes four. As he walks off with you on board in a relaxed manner, bridge and reinforce him again. Soon, standing still for mounting will be routine behavior for your horse.

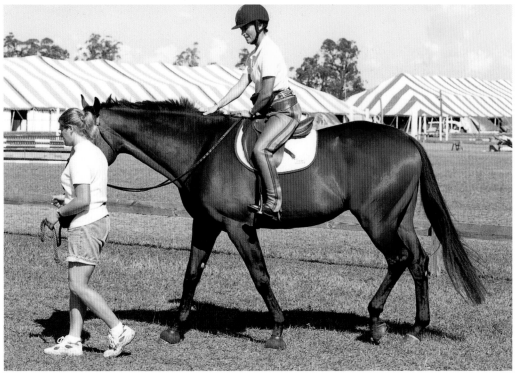

Your horse should be ready to be led at this point and your assistant should do the bridging and reinforcing. You want to work on walking, stopping, turning, and eventually trotting, progressing slowly and successfully through each stage. Repeat the process on the longe line with the rider mounted after the horse is cooperative about being led.

Getting accustomed to the feel of the rider using the reins comes next. To begin, you can gently remove the slack from the reins just before the ground assistant stops. To initiate steering, open the right rein straight out to the side just as the assistant is about to turn right. As you progress, your horse will learn to respond to cues from you, his rider. Soon, you will do the directing and also the bridging and reinforcing.

When you initially bridge and attempt to feed your horse from the saddle, he may not know what to do. If you find yourself in this position, gently use the rein to pull his head around to your outstretched hand. Your horse will adapt to being fed this way very easily.

As you shift the focus to the rider, you can subtract the halter, lead rope, and assistant. Keep these first sessions short. Build on them as you progress. Depending on how well your horse accepts the mounted work, the process could go very quickly or it could take a while. Pay attention to your horse. He will let you know how fast to move ahead. You don't want to overwhelm him or frighten him, and you don't want to bore him by moving too slowly. Generally, though, slower is better. The result is usually a more thoroughly trained horse. If your horse is not steady and relaxed, back up in your training. Remember that he'll need some time to build the muscle and balance required to carry your weight.

There are many good ways to train your horse to accept a rider. You can integrate On Target Training with any of them. The preceding approach has worked well for us. The idea is for you to consider the way I suggested starting the mounting process as a rough guideline. As you introduce your horse to saddle work, using the approach that works for you, remember to ignore undesired behavior as much as you can and draw attention to the behavior you want to see repeated by bridging and reinforcing desired behavior. We have also successfully integrated On Target Training with ground driving in long lines. Ground driving helps to teach a young horse about the rein-aids.

DE-SPOOKING AND BUILDING THE HORSE'S CONFIDENCE

Since horses are prey animals, they are born with a strong flight response. This innate response helps protect them from becoming a carnivore's meal. However, if this response goes unchecked, you can find yourself with a horse that's not safe to ride or possibly even be around. One of our goals as trainers is to minimize instinctive responses to alarming situations. Most of us have come across a horse who seems to react quite dramatically to objects and situations. What seems like an overreaction to us may seem quite reasonable to the horse. It's best to remain patient and focus on reducing fear. Remaining calm will go a long way toward defusing a difficult situation. Horses are herd animals and respond to the actions of those around them. The rider of a spooky horse tends to be braced for the worst; the horse is then more likely to react to this tension. Sometimes we encounter a horse that spooks to avoid work. This avoidance behavior is learned and can be replaced with more appropriate responses. As with training a horse under saddle, decreasing a horse's fear or avoidance involves a combination of traditional riding technique, common sense, and, of course, On Target Training.

The rider needs to minimize his response to spooky behavior and apply some common sense to solving fear response problems. If, for example, your horse tends to look out as you ride past the door of the indoor arena and then spook, prevent him from looking in that direction. Keep his focus elsewhere by bending him to the inside so he can't look out. When he passes the door without spooking, or even with less of a spook, bridge and reinforce. Once he is going by the door nicely, decrease the bend as you pass the doorway. If he responds well, bridge and reinforce again.

There are also ways to systematically teach horses about spooky objects and frightening noises. You can do this while riding or leading your horse. I would suggest starting on the ground. To initiate this process, equip yourself with a side-bucket, clicker, and target. Start the session in a familiar place such as the barn aisle, paddock, or indoor ring. Before the session, put something your horse would perceive as mildly frightening in your work area. A cooler or rug balled up and placed off to the side works well. As you walk your horse past this unfamiliar object, monitor his reaction. If he barely reacts, bridge and reinforce him near the item. If he has a dramatic reaction, keep walking steadily past without bridging and reinforcing. Then, reverse and walk past the cooler again. Should his reaction be even somewhat more subdued, bridge and reinforce when you are next to the cooler. If necessary in the beginning, use the target to get him to focus on something other than the cooler. Your horse will learn that he gets fed next to the strange object. Continue to repeat the exercise until he has little or no reaction. Signs of relaxation include a deep breath, licking the lips, and a relaxation of posture.

Next session, place a different object in the aisle. After this, do a session with yet another object in an alternative part of your work area. As you build on these sessions, you will find that your horse responds less to strange objects. When you observe this, repeat the process in a different place. When he's somewhere new, he may still occasionally get frightened. If so, use the target to encourage him to get near the new object. If your horse is the type who would normally avoid unfamiliar objects, let him look at and sniff the new item and then bridge and reinforce him for his inquisitive behavior. This process teaches him that unusual things are not necessarily threatening.

As your horse develops more confidence, stop allowing him to pause and examine new things. Bridge and reinforce him when he walks past an unusual object or for a relaxed approach. You will soon notice your horse observing new things without reacting to them (photos 89–92). Bridge and reinforce this behavior. It means he is making a choice to stay calm when confronted with a situation that formerly frightened him. This training process has taught him he's likely to be reinforced when he remains relaxed.

You can also condition your horse to adjust to unexpected or unusual movements from people. Start with a considerable distance between you and your horse, maybe with him in his stall and you on the other side of the aisle. Make small swinging movements with your arms. If he startles, keep swinging, wait until he settles, then bridge and reinforce. Continue with this process, increasing the scope of your movement and then decreasing the distance between you until you can do jumping jacks right in front of him.

It is impossible to completely eradicate a horse's fear response. Instead, we teach him to curb it. There will be times when something happens suddenly that surprises your horse. When this happens, as soon as he composes himself, bridge and reinforce.

This sort of work on the ground carries over to riding situations. When Mint was young, we worked with him in the barn aisle, teaching him to reduce his fear response. One day while we were at John and Beezie Madden's farm, a group of kids from the Pony Club came to visit. At the time, we were getting ready to do a demonstration in the indoor arena. I was walking Mint, who was two years old, from a separate barn to the indoor ring. Part of the training we do includes teaching our horses to follow us around the farm without a halter or lead line. As we entered the ring, the group of about twenty youngsters came running up, screaming and stomping the snow off their boots. Mint and I were both startled, but his response showed me how much he had learned. He jumped in place, splayed his feet, but did not leap away or stop what he was doing. He didn't even turn around to see the cause of the commotion and got right back to walking with me, nice and relaxed. Of course I bridged and reinforced him quite handsomely. This is exactly the response I would want if we were on the trail and a deer jumped out in front of us.

Follow the same procedure to curb spooking under saddle. Carry a waist pack filled with feed, place a cooler, rug, or similar object on a fence post or jump standard where you often ride your horse. Eventually build up to noisy objects that blow in the wind, but begin with something more subtle. Start at the walk to maximize control. Estimate how close you can get to this object without your horse reacting to it. If you think you can ride your horse within twenty feet of the object, make a circle that would take you twenty-two feet from the object you placed. When your horse passes the closest point to the object, bridge and reinforce. Next, circle a little closer to the object, perhaps by two feet. Bridge and reinforce again. In this exercise, it's important to set your horse up to succeed so you have the opportunity to reinforce correct behavior. To give your horse the best opportunity to succeed, progress slowly enough for him. He will learn that encountering a strange object calmly is likely to earn him food. The result will be a horse more willing to get close to new objects. Reinforce a relaxed attitude in a spooky situation. If you are riding past a frightening object and feel your horse tense, the second you feel him relax, bridge and feed him. Gradually increase the time between the instant he relaxes and the bridge. Whenever you notice your horse approaching an unfamiliar object in a relaxed manner, reinforce this action. The goal, after all, is not to get tense in the first place!

89-92 Brewster, shown in these photos, had a very spooky nature when I first bought him. In this sequence he comes out of the barn quietly, but then thinks twice about the lawn mower. You can see his attention shift from accompanying me, to worrying about the machine, so I calmly wait for him to make a decision about what he is going to do—run away, or stay with me. As soon as I have a clue it is going to be the latter, I continue on, then bridge and reinforce him as we pass closely by the lawn mower.

LESSONS UNDER SADDLE AND CANTER DEPARTS

Any under-saddle task is a conditioned response. You give a cue and your horse responds, no matter what your discipline or what you want your horse to accomplish. You can incorporate the On Target Training system to teach your horse any behavior, whether you want him to walk, trot, turn, lope, gallop, halt, jump, extend, cut cattle, spin, piaffe, stand while you open a gate, walk through water, or work without a bridle. Choose your goal. Break it down into small steps that build toward what you want to accomplish. Then plan how you can set your horse up to succeed. During the training process, continue what you established in your earlier work. Draw attention to desired behavior, as often as possible ignore unwanted behavior, and be flexible about your horse's rate of progress.

When Vinton and I train while riding, we wear a waist pack filled with feed such as pelleted grain or sugar cubes. (During under-saddle training, it's best to use something your horse likes that will easily dissolve in his mouth.) Initially, we use a clicker attached to a riding crop to bridge-signal. This helps free up our hands a little more. After a few weeks of training, when our horses clearly understand the significance of the bridge-signal from the rider, we replace the clicker with a verbal bridge-signal. We tried starting with a verbal bridge-signal but found that it slowed progress quite a bit. When they begin under-saddle work, experienced horses seem to go on automatic pilot. They tend not to pair the process they just learned with their work under saddle. When you apply On Target Training to a seasoned horse, the clicker's distinct sound communicates most clearly. Experienced horses can tune out the sound of the voice from the saddle; they may not connect a verbal bridge-signal with a reward until they've first come to recognize the sound of the clicker during the course of a few weeks. We found it better to begin bridging under saddle using a clicker.

• Teaching Canter Departs

Here is an example of how to train a particular under-saddle behavior. Vinton and I trained Mint to pick up correct canter leads integrating traditional methods with our system. You can easily integrate On Target Training with your system to teach any under-saddle behavior you wish.

When we began working with Mint, I was a green rider and he was a green horse. Vinton coached us from the ground so we could learn togeth-

93   As your horse becomes more used to being bridged and reinforced while being ridden, you can start to bridge-signal several times for correct responses before reinforcing him. You will need to continue your aids (or cues if you are not riding) after each bridge to maintain his forward movement, otherwise he will stop and expect his reward. You must still remember to reinforce often.

er. When we started working on canter departs, Mint knew how to pick up a canter, but not on a specific lead. He also knew the rudiments of bending and responding to leg and rein aids. Vinton helped me plan how to set Mint up to succeed in this endeavor, based on how we could integrate what Mint already knew with what we wanted to teach him. By adjusting his balance, I set him up so he was most likely to pick up the correct lead. I gave him my cue to canter. As soon as he began to pick up the correct lead, I bridged and reinforced. I bridged and stopped before Mint even cantered a full stride. I was not concerned about how long he cantered at that stage. Instead, I focused on his thought process. If Mint picked up the wrong lead, I stopped, rebalanced him, and again cued the canter depart. In between correct responses, we did other work such as trotting so Mint stayed loose and relaxed. Then I asked for a canter depart, varying the direction I traveled and the lead I requested. I repeated the process about eight times and allowed him to stop and eat when he responded correctly each time. I bridged the response I liked, which was the correct canter depart. After a few days of these sessions, Mint picked up the correct lead ninety percent of the time.

Once Mint was consistently picking up the correct lead, I had him add a few canter strides to the departs before I bridged. At first, I had to maintain the canter cue for an extra beat since he was accustomed to stopping after a correct depart. After a few strides, I bridged and reinforced. We had built up to cantering halfway around the ring after several days. The result of this effort was that after a week, Mint was solid on his canter departs. He never got anxious or tense. He focused instead on trying to figure out what I wanted so he could get reinforced. The On Target Training system expedited the process because it provided a way of communicating exactly what behavior I liked. There was something worthwhile in the endeavor for him.

Now, I rarely bridge and feed Mint for canter departs. He knows how to do them and he does them consistently. Every now and then, I bridge and reinforce a canter depart just to keep him guessing and motivated. We have continued to build on this chain of behaviors. I may ask for a canter depart, canter a circle, lengthen his stride down the long side of the ring, break to a trot, trot over a fence, pick up the other lead, and canter a circle. Then, I might bridge and reinforce.

Through this system, Mint has learned to be quite responsive and willing. By teaching these steps with On Target Training, you can build up to fifteen, twenty, or thirty minutes between reinforcement if you want to, or you could fade the food out. You can teach your horse to jump a course, ride a pattern, gallop a race, ride a test, go for a trail ride, or whatever goal you are working toward.

When training a new behavior, we found that it works best to bridge and reinforce often because we are raising the criteria. As you first teach your horse to continue on, you may need a little extra leg. When he responds correctly and continues, you can bridge that behavior. By doing so, you are teaching him a new concept. Once your horse consistently performs the behavior, you can bridge without having to reinforce each time. Let's say you're jumping a course. You feel your horse make an extraordinary effort. You want to communicate to him that you like this effort but you don't want to have him stop and eat yet. Bridge and keep your leg on, to tell him to continue going while pinpointing the desired behavior. It's a bit like working for a paycheck. You don't get paid every day but you know the check is coming so you continue to do a good job. I like to feed between sixty to sixty-five percent of my bridges, about one in three. Your horse's attitude will remain positive and the On Target Training will continue to expedite the training process.

ON THE TRAIL AND HACKING OUT

Taking your horse beyond the confines of a riding arena is important to his education. Begin by varying your riding locations to include paddocks, outdoor rings, indoor rings, fields, and finally, the trail. On the trail, you won't have to provide spooky objects; nature will provide plenty of stimuli. Keep the initial rides brief. Most horses are more comfortable going out with another horse. Try to find a quiet, steady trail companion. If the companion gets high-strung and excited, your horse may behave the same way. It may be better to start your horse alone than to take him out with this type of horse.

When horses are nervous on the trails, they usually react in one of two ways. They tend to be both apprehensive and reluctant to more forward or they prance and jig. In either circumstance, you will be looking and feeling for relaxation, no matter how slight. For the apprehensive, slow-to-move-forward horse, look for commitment to move forward. In the prancing horse, look for a more relaxed pace. Any improvement should be bridged and reinforced. On these rides, keep this On Target Training axiom in mind: bridge and reinforce the behavior you want to see repeated. Offer lots of reinforcement at first. If necessary for safety reasons, hand walk part of the way out. You can also dismount and hand walk your horse at particularly difficult spots on the trail. This will help build confidence. Continue to bridge and reinforce when your horse gets really good at passing strange objects and don't take it for granted when he shows no response in challenging circumstances. Instead, continue, on an occasional basis, to bridge and reinforce this trained, desirable behavior. Turning around to come home is usually very reinforcing. Treat it accordingly. Your horse should behave well when you turn around.

TRAINING THE THERAPEUTIC AND BEGINNER HORSE

When training a horse for a therapeutic riding program or beginning riders, your goal is quite different than when training a highly responsive performance horse. These horses will have to cope well with extraneous movement and activity. They often have to compensate for unbalanced and uncoordinated riders. In addition to these requirements, they need to have enough respect for their riders that as they progress, the horses respond appropriately. Good therapeutic riding horses are worth their weight in gold. They are truly special and don't often get the credit they deserve. Yet the horses who don't have the mentality to be trained for this job are in the minority, mainly high-strung or skittish horses. With the On Target Training system, many horses can be trained to do this well. You can teach your therapeutic-riding candidate or lesson-horse candidate to listen and respond to the ground trainer, as well as to the student, even when loose.

In the following discussion, my focus will be on the therapeutic riding horse for the disabled rider. These techniques are variations of the steps you would take to prepare a school horse for a beginning rider. First, focus on teaching the horse to be comfortable with rider balance and coordination problems, as well as sudden rider movements. Once he is trained, your horse should not find these aspects of his job startling or upsetting. This is a simple desensitization process, similar to those discussed earlier in the chapter. You can begin the process in several ways. You can be the rider, you can have someone else in the saddle, you can work with your horse on the longe line, or all of the above. When working on the longe line, the person doing the longeing should also do the bridging and reinforcing. When working with a rider in the saddle, the rider will do the bridging and reinforcing. Your training program will depend, at least somewhat, on your goal. If your eventual goal is to have a horse work off the longe line with a rider and respond to the ground trainer, start him on the longe line with a rider. Have the rider position himself slightly out of balance. If your horse continues along without changing his attitude, pace, or gait, bridge and reinforce from the ground.

If he changes how he goes, the rider should use the aids to get him back on an even keel and again shift out of balance. If there is less change in how the horse goes, bridge and reinforce. Continue the process until your horse is unaffected when the rider's balance changes. Ultimately, the rider should be able to lean back, forward, and from side to side. Bridge and reinforce correct responses. Add extraneous movements. The rider can start with arm swings and then swing her legs. Remember to bridge and reinforce the small steps along the way to the larger goal. Each step may seem huge to your horse. Repeat this work over several days or longer if your horse needs it. Off the longe, condition him to the presence of people walking alongside, as well as to a leader while the rider moves about in the saddle at the walk and trot. Refer to the section in Chapter Four on adding a second person to your training routine and adapt accordingly.

If you wish to have the horse respond to you as the ground trainer, you need to teach him verbal cues for walk, trot, canter, whoa, and a cluck for forward movement. Bridge and reinforce correct responses. When your horse complies with these cues on the longe, add a rider and give the cues again from the ground. In this circumstance, the rider becomes a prop for your horse to ignore while you give the cues. If he doesn't respond correctly, have the rider gently cue him using the traditional aids. If you ask for the trot and he doesn't respond, have the rider use his legs to encourage him forward. Continue until your horse responds solely to your voice without help from the rider.

A major component of training for therapeutic riding is desensitizing horses to unusual sounds, objects, and actions. Most of these will come into play during the mounting process. Some riders have wheelchairs, crutches, or braces. The process itself is not likely to be smooth or fluid because of their various disabilities. Use the object-desensitization techniques described earlier to condition your horse. Include desensitization training for the unusual sounds of the equipment, such as falling crutches. As always, bridge and reinforce correct responses. Before introducing your horse to the platform area used for mounting, desensitize him to objects like ramps and platforms in a place where he has room to move. Once he is relaxed, work with him in the mounting area. Refer to this chapter's earlier section on mounting to accustom your horse to accepting riders getting on his back. You can easily adapt these directions to the specialized mounting platform usually used in therapeutic programs. Keep in mind that the mounting process should be as comfortable for your horse as for the disabled riders. The edges of the wheelchair-access ramp should be padded and rounded off to eliminate sharp edges. The footing should be appropriate to help your horse better keep his balance. These extra efforts will make the process far more comfortable and inviting for your horse and will ultimately make the experience a more rewarding one for the riders.

When you can put different riders on his back and he responds correctly on a consistent basis, your horse is a serious candidate for a therapeutic riding program. As with all training, there are many approaches to developing a good therapeutic riding horse. Any of these methods will become more effective by integrating On Target Training.

Horses in elementary riding-lesson programs can also benefit from adding On Target Training to their routine. Most beginning riders lack a sense of timing and feel when giving or softening their aids, which can result in a horse developing a sour attitude toward his work. However, when a horse is trained through our system, the trainer on the ground can use a bridge-signal to reward the horse's correct responses just as they occur. The rider can then reinforce the horse. This process allows the horses to maintain a good attitude and the rider to develop a sense of timing and feeling and become a better equestrian as a result.

SETTING YOUR HORSE UP TO SUCCEED IN SOLVING UNDER-SADDLE PROBLEMS

You can help your horse overcome his under-saddle problems if you take the steps, as always, to *set him up to succeed.* If your horse is unwilling to move forward, you may want to ride him before he's turned out for initial work on solving this problem. Hopefully, he'll then expend his energy constructively in the training session rather than while turned out. This will provide you more opportunities to reinforce him. When you ride him, bridge and reinforce each little *upward* transition and the slightest forward response to your aids. Start by bridging and reinforcing his transition from standing to walking, walking to trotting, and then trotting to cantering. As he gets the idea, extend the time between bridges. Within a few weeks, also bridge correct *downward* transitions to build his responsiveness.

Conversely, if your horse bolts or is too quick or nervous, you may want to set him up to succeed by turning him out before riding him so he can release excess or nervous energy. With this type of horse, start by bridging downward transitions, relaxation, and collection. Start by bridging the walk to halt, repeat a few times, progress from trot to walk, and eventually, work on the transition from canter down to the trot. If your horse is adept at longeing, you may want to start these lessons on a longe line without a rider. When the horse responds well, you can add a rider. Once the rider has developed a reinforcement-history with him, remove the longe line so he can focus solely on the rider. (These are guidelines or suggestions. You should adapt the program to your situation and consider the experience level of both the horse and rider.)

Ultimately, you'll be able to fade-out the use of these tools for success from your horse's training program once you've had the opportunity to reinforce him for the behavior you want. The result of this training will be a more motivated horse with a better understanding of what is expected of him.

Sometimes, a nervous horse isn't comfortable eating when he's being ridden. If your horse is too nervous to eat, use the following approach. Once he's bridge-conditioned and target-trained, take him for walks in the ring where you normally work him, using just a halter and lead rope. Bring a clicker, a target, and food. Use these tools to teach him it's all right to eat while walking around the riding ring. When he's relaxed, add his saddle and repeat the process. When he's comfortable, add a rider too, but just continue to lead with a halter and lead rope. At first, the person leading him should bridge and reinforce. Then progress to having the rider bridge and reinforce. Adding the bridle comes next, with the halter and lead rope over it. Go through the same steps until you can remove the halter and lead rope and the rider can take over without an increase in nervousness. The rider should start by feeding him at the walk. You can progress to trotting once he's very comfortable at the walk. When you've succeeded in getting him to eat, you've come a long way toward repairing his fractious attitude. You'll find that the pace of the training process will increase because you have begun to build trust.

Feeding does a lot toward the goal of calmness. It triggers physical reactions that enhance relaxation. When you ride a nervous horse, bridge and reinforce him anytime you feel him unwind. This will teach him to connect the concept of eating with relaxation. This concept is incompatible with bolting and nervous behavior. Once horses begin learning to relax, you can usually begin to remove equipment you've used to restrain or limit their movement. Take your time when resolving these problems. There is no such thing as a long-lasting quick fix.

I've outlined a few of the basic problems we frequently encounter. Once your horse understands the bridge-signal and the target, you have the basic tools to teach him anything or to undo any problem. You can easily adapt these guidelines to your specific problem or discipline. There is a way to reshape just about any behavior. Establish your goals. Then, study your horse's tendencies, identify what he finds reinforcing, and plan the small steps you can take to achieve your goal and set your horse up to succeed. Often when you resolve problems, you are actually breaking a habit the horse has developed. We know how hard it can be to break ingrained habits. By giving your horse some motivation, and doing what you can to ensure his success, you can change his behavior. If your horse is making even a little progress, you're on the right track! Continue your efforts and maintain your patience.

GOOD DECISIONS UNDER SADDLE

You can address any riding issue using On Target Training. I couldn't possibly address all the possible problems people contend with throughout the various disciplines, so I'll address a few of the most common ones. Tailor your training program with the On Target Training principles to solve any problems you may encounter. However, solving some problems may require the help of a good professional. If you have any doubt about your ability to resolve a riding problem, don't hesitate to get professional assistance (see Chapter Six for more on seeking the help of professionals).

When dealing with problem behaviors, it's important to first determine whether the difficulty has a physical cause. Confirm that the saddle and other tack fit the horse well. Then, consult your veterinarian to find out if pain or discomfort is causing your horse's troubled behavior. If so, treat him until he's healed before proceeding. Once he is physically healed, resume your work. Physical healing may not eliminate the problem right away. Your horse may anticipate the return of the pain that originally caused his incorrect behavior and may now associate a particular movement or rider request with his discomfort. So build slowly and reinforce good steps toward your goal. If you observe a pattern to your horse's behavior, make a note of it. For example, he may buck or kick out every time he goes by the gate or bulge out when going toward the barn. Something about his behavior must be reinforcing, otherwise he wouldn't do it. If you recognize his pattern or any external stimuli that contribute to his behavior, you can figure this out. Identifying his patterns will help fix the problem. If your horse exhibits undesirable patterns on the longe line, you can start working with him there to keep you safer while you start to build a correct reinforcement-history. Your goal is to make it more reinforcing to behave correctly.

Bucking, rearing, bolting, and the like are usually evasive behaviors. Horses that display these problem actions have most likely become frustrated and are now taking desperate and dangerous measures to avoid work and such aversives such as leg, bit, whip, spur, or perhaps even the rider. Often these tactics work, if only for the short term. If the rider gets off the horse when he behaves this way, the horse gets out of work by intimidating the rider, using removal-reinforcement to his advantage.

There was a situation where a horse was having a problem at the canter. He started to buck when asked for a canter depart. The rider got off each time and longed the horse. The behavior increased in frequency. Soon, he was bucking at the trot and eventually at the walk. He had learned this great new way to get his rider off his back. To stop this behavior, the rider's trainer, who was a skilled, confident rider, began working with the horse. She started at the walk and rode the bucking out. Eventually, the horse learned that this ploy no longer worked and he stopped putting all that effort into bucking. By looking at this from the horse's perspective and realizing what is reinforcing the behavior, you can more effectively teach your horse and perhaps avoid creating similar scenarios in the first place.

Consider for a moment what motivates your horse to behave well. In traditional training, it's removal-reinforcement—the removal of aversives. Behavioral scientists have proven that this approach may create frustration. When you use reward-reinforcement, the horse is rewarded when he behaves well, avoiding most of these unpleasant and dangerous situations. The old adage about an ounce of prevention being the best cure holds true.

Use a variation of the following step-by-step process to solve any unwanted under-saddle behavior. I'll focus on bucking by the in-gate as the undesired behavior you want to change. If your horse is competent at longeing, you may want to start on the longe line. Begin by longeing your horse at the problem area. Start at the walk since you're more likely to be successful at this gait. Bridge and reinforce as your horse walks past the gate calmly. If he bucks, keep going until he walks correctly. Bridge and reinforce when he shows any improvement, even a slight improvement. Look for relaxation. You may bridge and reinforce at other times also, but

I would recommend that you focus mainly on bridging him for being calm in this area. Progress to longeing at the trot and canter in the same manner. Change direction and repeat the process. Take your time. It may take a few days. We are rehabilitating his psyche much the same way you would rehabilitate a physical problem. Build up slowly. Seeing improvement means you're on the right track. When he is going well and has established a good reinforcement-history, you can add a rider, but keep the horse on the longe line just using the rider as a "prop." You—the person longeing—should still do the bridging and reinforcing. When the horse goes well in both directions, allow the rider to bridge and reinforce while you longe. This will shift the focus back to the rider. Start slowly, reinforcing correct behavior at the walk, the trot, and then the canter. When he behaves correctly, prepare for the next step.

Start the next session with you longeing and reinforcing, as above. If the horse goes well in each direction, eliminate the longe line and have the rider take over the cues as well as the reinforcing. Have the rider follow the same track, and proceed in the same manner as before when she was being longed.

When you get back in the saddle, focus on bridging and reinforcing when he passes the gate, sometimes as he approaches the gate, and sometimes several strides after the gate. If he reverts to bucking, focus on keeping his head up, as well as your own, and keep him moving forward to minimize his ability to buck. Keeping your own head up increases your ability to stay balanced and reduce the likelihood of a fall. Then, take a step back in the training to build up his reinforcement-history so he will want to do his job. This process, when used consistently, should serve to eliminate bucking or other undesirable behavior.

Other problems such as balking, spinning, and bolting are dealt with in a similar way. In the case of rearing, keep your horse moving forward since this is incompatible with rearing. Whatever you do, don't tug on the reins. Pulling on the reins encourages rearing. If you pull at the peak of a rear, you can pull him off balance. Grab the mane instead. For rearing and balking problems, bridge and reinforce upward transitions to encourage forward movement. Begin with a halt-to-walk transition, then move up from the walk to the trot, and then from the trot to the canter. Your horse will stop when he's bridged, but he will remember which behavior earned him the bridge-signal. Since we are building up his attitude and reinforcement-history here, keep the sessions short and successful to start.

CIBOR'S STORY

To illustrate how well On Target Training transforms "no" to "yes," I'd like to share with you a story of a horse whose motivation and under-saddle performance changed dramatically with the addition of On Target Training to his education. Cibor, a Dutch Warmblood gelding, changed from performing in any but the most perfunctory way, plodding along as dully and lazily as he could get away with, to working with joy and enthusiasm. After only a few weeks of On Target Training, this Dutch horse became walking, trotting, and cantering proof that you can train "heart" into a horse that has lost it. His dressage test scores went up an average of ten points and he's progressed from the lower end of class placings to winning at big, rated shows.

This horse's owner usually enjoyed turning difficult horses into successful amateur show horses, but this upper-level dressage prospect's unwillingness to cooperate was more of a challenge than she expected. Cibor ignored the leg aids she gave him, even when supplemented with a spur or whip. The owner consulted with her veterinarian and after an evaluation, ruled out physical problems as an explanation for his unwillingness to work. Even cross-country gallops, trail rides, and jumping did little to enthuse him or motivate him to go forward. The owner worked with a grand-prix rider, who initially suggested bigger spurs and a longer whip. But the owner and the trainer found that those aids worked only temporarily to encourage forward movement. Although he could feel a fly landing on his flanks and would flick it off with his tail, Cibor was desensitized to the whip and spurs. By the time I met with them, both owner and trainer had tried everything they could think of to convince this horse to cooperate, to no avail. It looked as though the brilliant dressage movement this horse was born with was going to waste because he was such a reluctant student.

When the owner told me about her horse's issues, I was sure he could improve with On Target Training. Based on what she told me, I was confident I could resolve his motivational problem. At the time we spoke, the owner was on the verge of giving up on forging a partnership with Cibor and was looking at other horses, so time was of the essence. We wanted to do things at a quicker pace than usual. Although I prefer to spend a week doing the initial training, we condensed his introduction to On Target Training to three days. (I don't recommend such a shortcut under normal circumstances.)

First I worked on bridge-conditioning. When we approached Cibor's stall, he was quietly eating hay. I loaded my side-bucket with Sweet Lumps, a treat I was told he enjoyed, and entered. The first thing I learned about this horse was that he was very responsive and interested in people to the point of being a little pushy in his demands for attention. As soon as I went in to bridge-condition him, my priority was to get him to stop pushing me or pushing at my side-bucket to get to the food, which is a normal reaction in the first training session. He didn't understand why I wasn't putting the food I brought into his stall into his feed tub. The first thing I set out to teach him was to look away from the side-bucket instead. I also wanted him to keep a bit of distance from me, so I waited until he first looked away before I bridged. I waited until he looked away again, and bridged. By the third time he looked away, he bent his neck away from me but still watched me. His behavior was already deliberate. After hearing the click and getting a reward, he turned his head even further away from me. He quickly got the idea that there was a reason for getting the food reward, just as the domineering German warmblood I described in Chapter Three had.

This was Cibor's first lesson in learning to respect my space. Once I saw him consistently give me space, the objective of the lesson was accomplished. Now, on to the next lesson, which was teaching him to maintain eye contact by bridging and reinforcing that action. This results, as Cibor's story illustrates, in a horse who watches and focuses on you without crowding you.

I next bridged and fed Cibor when he both looked toward me and stood still. I would recommend bridging when horses hold still because it teaches them to focus on you and be patient. Although some people might think this practice would have the opposite effect, bridging in this manner actually helps curb active begging behavior such as pawing and nudging. Horses soon learn that they are rewarded for standing still.

I worked with him that night about five minutes and then left and stood outside the stall doorway, talking with his owner. He started nudging and pushing over the stall door to get attention. I either ignored this behavior or quickly moved away. I wanted him to learn that's not the way to get attention. After that episode, he stopped the pushy behavior toward me and I made a point of reinforcing his behavior with food when he stood quietly and attentively.

The next day, I returned to the barn to repeat the same bridging process for five-minute sessions in both morning and afternoon. By the third session, it was clear that Cibor was anticipating food when he heard the clicker.

That evening, twenty-four hours after being introduced to the bridge-signal, I introduced him to the target. (Again, I don't ordinarily recommend proceeding this quickly. It's far better to take more time to establish a solid foundation.) On the third day that I worked with Cibor, he was showing signs of comprehending his new program, so the owner and I decided to take advantage of a scheduled lesson she was having with a dressage professional the following day to start under-saddle work. The goal for this horse was to move forward when his rider asked. Without a doubt, this was going to be the most unusual lesson this grand-prix dressage rider ever taught. The three of us talked about the lesson plan as Cibor was tacked up. (Whatever your discipline, it's helpful if you are working with a professional and having lessons to clue him or her in on what you're doing.) Like Cibor's owner, this trainer was at her wit's end, trying to come up with ways to encourage this horse to go forward. The traditional methods hadn't worked and she was willing to try On Target Training. The plan, we agreed, was basic: to encourage Cibor to go forward.

We weren't expecting dramatic results in the first session. I attached a clicker to the top of the owner's dressage whip, and she filled her vest pocket with sugar cubes and other small treats Cibor could comfortably chew while wearing a bridle. The plan was to bridge even the slightest response. When she pressed her leg against Cibor's sides and he responded by moving forward, the owner was to bridge and reinforce that behavior.

The owner got on and asked him to walk forward with a squeeze of her legs. When he responded, she pressed the clicker, then leaned forward to offer him a sugar cube. At first the gelding wasn't sure how to eat from the rider's hand. However, from the first moment the rider clicked and offered food, she had her horse's complete attention, which lasted throughout the lesson. She received an upward transition the majority of times she asked for one, constantly bridging and offering reinforcement.

We were all delighted to see a rapid change in this horse's attitude. Instead of exerting himself as little as he could, now he was trying to figure out what to do to earn a reward. We kept this first session brief, ending the lesson after barely a half hour once Cibor offered forward transitions from the trot to the canter in each direction.

Within a few weeks, the owner found herself on a "new" horse. Now that he was being reinforced for correct behavior, Cibor leaped into his upward transitions and seemed eager to perform what was asked of him. His behavior was reported to me by telephone; six weeks after I worked with this horse, I returned to see his progress. I was a little concerned that I might not recognize the nuances of this horse's improvement without an extensive dressage background. However, the change was quite obvious and dramatic. When I had first watched Cibor work, he seemed rather clunky and dull. His tail swished in annoyance when his owner asked him to go forward. Now, he was bright and powerful. The difference was really exciting. Even the way he held his tail was different: elevated, but steady and relaxed.

A primary goal of On Target Training is to teach people to influence their horses' behavior through reward. While seeing Cibor's attitude and performance change was satisfying, what is most rewarding for me is the owner's enthusiasm about this training program's effect on her horse's behavior. I knew the horse would improve. What I enjoy most is watching people become enlightened and realize, as this owner did, the many applications for this training. She has since used On Target Training to decrease spooking on the trail and to teach him to stand quietly for clipping. Beyond solving the problem behavior, the possibilities are endless, the lessons priceless. After all, who will be teaching this horse on a daily basis? It won't be me. It will be his owner who trains him, just as you train your horse.

CHAPTER

Problem Solving

ost horses, no matter how well trained or how talented, harbor habits or behaviors we wish would disappear. These undesirable behaviors vary in severity. Some may be little more than annoying, while others range up to the level of highly dangerous. No matter which end of the behavior spectrum your horse's undesirable actions fall under, the approach to solving these problems will be the same.

To start, we need to attempt to understand the behavior in question and think about why the horse is behaving in such a way. Everything a horse does is either to avoid or attain something in his environment. This capacity to learn begins the day he is born, when he figures out how to get milk while avoiding being stepped on by his dam. As he grows, he learns how to avoid wind when it's cold and how to find shade when it's hot. There are countless numbers of environmental factors that a horse figures out affect him. We are a significant part of our horse's life and figure strongly in the environmental equation.

As I've explained before, if a behavior increases in frequency, that behavior is being reinforced by something in the horse's environment. The reinforcement the horse receives may be delivered quite unintentionally. What we perceive as a reinforcing or even a disciplinary action may be perceived in a very different way by your horse. Here's an example.

A horse I became familiar with had the annoying habit of pawing while standing on the cross-ties. The cross-ties were located outside a fairly large barn. The tack and grooming supplies were kept inside a nearby bungalow. Whenever the groom went inside to get tack or supplies, the horse would paw. The groom tried to correct this problem by quickly coming out of the building and scolding him. This action had no effect on the pawing, so she escalated the discipline by coming out of the bungalow and striking the horse with a riding crop. Can you guess the result of this action? The more severe discipline did not have the effect the groom hoped it would. Instead, the pawing got worse.

The groom thought she was being quite clear to the horse that he was being punished for his pawing behavior. The horse's perspective was very different. He was more concerned about being left alone than he was by what the groom did to him when she returned. He would rather have her there with him, even though she was obviously displeased with him, than be alone. He learned, while being on the cross-ties, that if he pawed his groom returned very quickly. The solution to this problem was a simple one based on our axiom of ignoring undesirable behavior and drawing attention to correct behavior. To stop the pawing, the groom needed to remain in the tack bungalow, ignore the pawing, and maximize her own potential as a reinforcer by coming out of the building only when he was standing without pawing. In doing so, she taught the horse that when he exhibited undesirable behavior—the pawing—nothing happened. However, if he stood quietly and did not paw, his groom returned to him. This lesson could be enhanced, of course, by adding in a bridge-signal to communicate correct behavior and food to accentuate the reward-reinforcement of the groom's presence.

Don't be overly concerned when your horse makes incorrect decisions. It's part of the process of how he learns to make correct decisions. If you find your horse repeatedly making incorrect decisions in the same situation, back up a few steps in training to make sure he isn't confused or receiving unintentional reinforcement for undesired behavior.

SEEKING PROFESSIONAL HELP

There are times when even experienced horsepeople need the help of a professional. There are many great trainers out there and plenty of constructive ways to eliminate unwanted or dangerous behavior. Don't hesitate to seek help or advice. Most problematic horse behavior has been inadvertently taught by humans. Sometimes it comes from too much discipline, sometimes, not enough. If you have the slightest doubt about managing your horse's behavior, get the help of a professional. Adding a second pair of experienced eyes can help spot a problem you may be overlooking.

There are plenty of good trainers. Unfortunately, there are also unethical trainers out there as well, so the best way to find the right professional is to gather as much information as you can before making a choice. Talk with the person who will actually be doing the training. Learn about his training philosophies and ask what procedures will be followed. Ask how long the training will take. Then ask yourself if you agree with that person's training ideas. Does his plan make sense to you? If not, it probably won't make sense to your horse. Ask if you can watch the trainer work with a horse. Does what happens in the work session make sense to you? Is the trainer practicing what he preaches? Is he using undue adversives? How is the horse responding? Does he seem content and willing, or does he seem irritated and frustrated? Are his ears forward and expression bright or does he have his ears pinned or wear a shy, fearful expression? The horse's body language can tell you a lot. The answers to all these questions can tell you a lot about a trainer.

It's also important for you to be involved with the training process. At the very minimum, you should watch so you can understand the steps the trainer is taking to undo your horse's undesirable behavior. Be certain that you can follow through and are comfortable applying his techniques. A large and often-forgotten step in retraining is following through with the process.

Let's say your horse bolts on the way to the paddock. At that instant, he is dangerous to you and to himself, so you want him to learn to walk in a mannerly fashion. So you send him away to a professional for training. He comes back and behaves perfectly going to and from the paddock. Then, when you go to board out at a different farm, the behavior problem recurs. If you know the steps that were taken by the professional, you can easily get him back on track before the problem escalates. If you don't, you are out of luck.

I have heard many complaints from people who have sent their horses away only to find that training eventually comes undone. For this reason, we always include the owner, or whoever handles or rides the horse, in our training sessions. You can never be sure exactly what triggers undesirable behavior in the first place. Sometimes, out of the blue, a horse will revert back to his old habits. As long as you know the training steps and can execute them, you can get his behavior back to a desirable level. So plan to participate in your horse's training.

EXERCISE CAUTION

Unlike relatively benign forms of unwanted behavior such as pawing, activity that has the potential to injure or harm the horse himself, other horses, or the people around your horse, must be dealt with decisively and immediately. In the case of *dangerous* behavior, the On Target Training axiom of ignoring unwanted behavior and drawing attention to desired actions simply does not apply. Do not ignore any behavior that poses an immediate threat to you or anyone else, but do what is necessary to stop it. For example, if you are in your horse's stall picking out manure and he pins his ears and comes at you in an aggressive manner to bite, you must use whatever means necessary to protect yourself. This will probably include some abrupt aversive stimulus, possibly your foot, your hand, or a nearby tool. When this occurs, keep in mind the behavior you want from him. If you want him to turn his head away from you, cease using the aversive stimulus when he performs this desired behavior so you communicate effectively which behavior is correct. Remember to look for opportunities to reinforce your horse when he acts appropriately.

There are numerous situations that can be perceived as dangerous, although many horses are bluffers. It's not always easy to distinguish one situation from the other, especially with an unfamiliar horse, or if you are unused to horses. If you are a novice, becoming familiar with horses and their behavior may take a while. I recommend that when you begin riding or spending time around them, you do so alongside a good, experienced horse person who can help you learn safely. Also take advantage of print and video resources to expand your equine education.

It always makes sense to exercise caution around horses and other large animals, particularly in new situations. After all, no matter how well-trained, quiet, or familiar, horses have great potential to harm us and themselves even unintentionally. Respect their size and strength.

Most unwanted or dangerous behaviors stem from frustration, fear, or panic. Incorporating reward-reinforcement and going slowly with your training process will help to minimize frustration. Studies have shown that use of reward-reinforcement increases the safety factor by minimizing frustration. By training this way, you allow a horse to make choices; therefore, he does not feel trapped or coerced. This eliminates the fear, or even panic that can be associated with using removal-reinforcement alone. Flight animals such as horses will go to great lengths to defend themselves if they perceive a strong enough threat. It doesn't take much to panic them. However, by allowing your horse to make choices, you greatly reduce the panic response.

IMPROVING STALL MANNERS

The origin of bad stall manners can vary. Usually, bad stall manners have their roots in aggressive behavior such as charging, biting, or turning to kick. Sometimes these behaviors arise out of defensiveness. The horse may feel cornered. He may feel he can't flee and isn't comfortable with someone in his stall. Perhaps the behavior arises when a second person enters his stall, which could make him suspect he will have to endure veterinary procedures. It could stem from extreme fear if the horse won't let you touch or catch him in his stall. Others just behave territorially about their stalls as if the stall is the only place that's theirs and they want to get rid of anyone who enters their domain.

In all the above scenarios, the behavior is probably being reinforced through removal-reinforcement. Recall the story in the early part of the book about Hershey, the show hunter. This behavior started with him not wanting unfamiliar people in his stall. Hershey was also reinforced through reward-reinforcement when the staff dumped his food and got out of his stall as quickly as possible, providing him both the privacy he wanted and his dinner. In this type of situation, we must build up the horse's positive association with us, his handlers.

If a horse behaves very aggressively, it may be dangerous to enter his stall. In this case, start bridge-conditioning while outside the stall, through the bars, or with the door open six-to-eight inches. Do not bridge or feed him when he looks aggressive or irritated. Wait until he looks relaxed and has his ears pricked forward. Bridging only the behavior you want him to repeat will shape his attitude. His irritable attitude may have been inadvertently been trained at feeding time, as with Hershey. If necessary, feed him yourself for a while or have the person feeding him use the On Target Training program and explain what behavior to bridge. Continue to bridge and reinforce when the horse looks pleasant. If he continues to look hostile, close the stall door and walk away for a few minutes. Then try again. Remember to keep the door closed enough to keep you protected while you work with him.

Usually, you'll see a substantial improvement in your horse even in the first session. When he seems consistently relaxed in your presence, open the door further, then bridge and reinforce him when he exhibits a good attitude. Next, step inside his stall. If he is still relaxed, bridge and reinforce him and if he remains pleasant, put the balance of his feed in his grain bucket.

Keep these sessions very reinforcing in the beginning. You don't want him to get frustrated. Once you observe initial progress, increase your focus to include appropriate manners as well. Begin with expecting him to stand quietly between bridges and slowly build up the time between these bridges. If he continues to respond well, move on to target-training with a hand-held and then a stationary target. At this point, the horse will look forward to you coming into his stall and will no longer perceive you as a threat.

If the horse continues to behave aggressively, start target-training through the bars or door of the stall, again looking for opportunities to reinforce a good attitude. When you add the target in this situation, you are reinforcing him for doing something constructive as opposed to exhibiting undesired behavior. (The technique to replace one behavior with another—**differential reinforcement of incompatible behavior [DRI]** follows later in the chapter.) When he targets well, extend the target further in, hold it high, then low, and next begin to slowly offer the target as you start to come into the stall. I would then teach him to touch and hold on a stationary target, which will help him focus further on making appropriate responses. Once the horse allows you to enter and exit his stall in a relaxed manner, work to maintain this behavior. Go in his stall a few times a week and work with him; perhaps teach him new behaviors such as a bow or leg lifts. (See Chapter Seven for "Just-for-Fun" Behaviors.) Continue to monitor his attitude at feeding time to be sure he's not acting unpleasantly when he's fed.

SEPARATION ANXIETY

This problem tends to show up in horses who have spent much of their time with either a constant companion or in a herd. Horses can become nervous or excitable when separated from the safe and familiar. The solution to this problem is to teach our horses to trust us and to understand that unpleasant things don't happen when they're alone away from friends. We can show them that good things can happen instead.

First, I'll focus on teaching a horse to separate from a herd and learn to live in a stall. In the case of a youngster getting ready to begin his working life, begin with brief separations in proximity to the other horses to minimize anxiety and panic. An adjacent paddock where he can still see the others is ideal. If necessary, work him just outside his paddock. The steps will vary, depending on your situation. If possible, start at feeding time and separate your horse only to eat. This will go a long way toward building up a good, strong association with separation. As soon as he's finished his meal, before he's had a chance to panic, return him to the herd. Begin to build on this experience by feeding him further away from the others, gradually increasing the distance. An additional benefit of this training is that your horse will learn to eat in different places.

Another approach might be to hand-feed him. This works well for a horse attached to his companions. While you're feeding him, his confidence in your presence will increase. Start by standing just outside his usual living space, whether it's a stall or a paddock. Next, begin walking and feeding, leading him a bit further away. Walk in small circles. Bridge and reinforce as he's going away from the others. Keep in mind that going back toward the group is its own reinforcement. Utilize bridge-conditioning and target-training to help him stay focused. If he already knows the bridge and target routines, start teaching him a new behavior while he's separated. Keep these sessions short and sweet. If you can, feed him all his meals while he's separated. This will be a significant building block in his reinforcement-history. Slowly build up the time he's away from his companions. We found that increasing reinforcement by using On Target Training, horses quickly begin to look forward to their training sessions, no matter where they take place.

Next, I'll address separating horses that are bonded to each other. To reduce anxiety, feed two buddies their meals while they're separated. Or work with your horse in his stall while the other horse is out, if that's when he becomes anxious. Keep the separation brief at first and build up the time span. Perhaps progress to doing three short sessions with your horse while his friend is gone. Do a session, step out of his stall and wait a few minutes, and if he's standing quietly, return for another session. You'll be able to build up the time between sessions and reduce the time in the stall. The next step is to simply reinforce him from outside his stall when he's standing quietly. Slowly build on this behavior and vary the amount of reinforcement. Sometimes, feed him a lot. Sometimes, feed him a small amount. Use other things he likes as reinforcement such as toys, or physical contact if he likes being rubbed or scratched. Remember to draw attention to correct behavior and ignore undesired behavior.

Another powerful reinforcer in these circumstances is the presence of the other horse. Be aware of what your horse does when he is allowed to rejoin his friend. You can actually train in superstitious behavior. Let's say you take the buddy away and your horse starts to act up. You then bring the buddy back right away. Your horse's misbehavior may be reinforced by the reappearance of his friend. However, if the buddy comes back only when your horse is quiet, he will learn that the action of standing quietly is the one key to his friend's return.

Be aware of this process with paddock behavior. If your horse starts running or pacing and you bring him in, soon, he will have trained you! If he is reinforced for running by getting to return to the barn, he may very well repeat the behavior the next time he wants to come indoors.

BUILDING CONFIDENCE OVER FENCES

One problem specific to horses who jump is stopping in front of a fence. This behavior is both dangerous and frustrating. As with all problems, the specific details of a refusal may vary. Accordingly, approaches with various horses who refuse will vary. Usually, stopping stems from a confidence issue. The horse may not be confident in himself or in his rider.

First, we prefer to build the horse's confidence by teaching him to jump on his own. We do this with green horses so they learn to negotiate jumps independently, and with experienced horses to solve problems such as stopping or rushing to the fence. In either situation, teaching horses to jump through the On Target Training method builds relaxation, confidence, and boldness. When we teach free jumping, we start by having the horse go from point A, where there is a person with a target, to point B, where another person waits with a target. The people at points A and B also have clickers and food for reinforcement. We begin by establishing the two points being five feet apart. Gradually, we increase the distance until the points are seventy-five to one hundred feet apart. The horse starts at point A. The point A person points to the person at point B and says,

"Go." The person at point B calls the horse's name and presents the target. As the horse goes toward point B, the person at point B bridges and then reinforces, feeding the horse a couple of handfuls of food when he arrives. Then, the ground person at B repositions the horse to go back to point A. During the training process, pay attention to bridging and reinforcing while the horse stays at point B to avoid his anticipating heading back to point A. Reinforce handsomely when he returns to the other point person at A with energy, since he will need that energy when a jump is added to the exercise.

Next, put two jump standards with a rail on the ground between them. At this stage, set point A and point B about ten feet apart on either side of the jump. Bridge as he steps over the pole. By timing your bridge this way, you draw attention to his action of crossing the pole. Once, we had to put a halter and lead rope on a horse and get behind him and cluck to get him over the pole. As he performed the correct behavior—stepping over the pole—we bridged and reinforced him. After a few passes this way, we removed the halter and lead rope. As we expected, he remembered the action that got him reinforced and stepped over the pole on his own. Usually, horses don't have difficulty stepping over poles on the ground, but do what is necessary to set your horse up for success and then fade-out that tool. The next step is to establish point A and point B further apart. Continue sending your horse from one point to the other and bridge when he goes between the jump standards and crosses over the ground rail.

Sometime during the training, your horse will try to go around the jump. This is part of his learning process. When he does this, give him a three-second pause when he returns to you, offer no reinforcement, and resend him. If he continues to go around the jump, move points A and B closer together again and build up from there.

After your horse is adept at this, turn two poles into a small cross-rail; put one side of the rail into the jump cup at the lowest position on the standard. Set the other side of the rail on the ground. Add another pole the same way on the other side to form a very low X. Send your horse over the small jump until he goes back and forth comfortably (photos 94 and 95). Slowly increase the criteria for success by raising the cross-rail one hole at a time. Eventually place a rail straight across the two standards to make a vertical jump. Be sure to place ground rails on each side of the jump, and as the jump gets a little higher, move the rails out a bit further

94-95   I am pointing Mint toward Vinton who is on the left out of the picture to teach him to walk across a small jump. Vinton bridges Mint the moment he lifts his left leg up to step across (top photo). He reinforces Mint as soon as he arrives.

to help your horse evaluate when to leave the ground. This will help your horse in the early stages of jumping. Remove the ground rails as your horse becomes more advanced. Remember to allow him sufficient starting and stopping room as the exercise progresses (photos 96–98).

The aerial behaviors you see at Sea World such as bows, jumps, and flips are all taught with targets. Their initial behaviors look nothing like the finished product. You start by guiding them with the target but you shape the behavior with selective bridging. Likewise with horses. Once your horse is jumping consistently, bridge and reinforce the action you like and give a three-second pause with no reinforcement for the performance you don't like. Your horse will quickly figure out which behavior earns him reinforcement. When shaping a behavior, work on one thing at a time for the sake of clarity. Let's say you want your horse to lift his knees and you also want him to lower his head while jumping. Work on one thing first. When he achieves the first goal, focus on the second one.

Now, let's say you have your horse successfully jumping two-feet, six inches and perhaps jumping a line of fences. Next add a saddle and when he is successfully free jumping with a saddle, add a rider. At this stage, the rider is only a "prop." Put the poles back down to the ground and send him from point A to point B. Move up slowly, reinforcing each step as you build a reinforcement-history with the weight of this rider added. Early in the process, the people standing at the two points should continue to do the reinforcing and the horse and rider should stand still at point A until the person at point B calls them over the jumps (photos 99–101). Progress to having the rider do the reinforcing and slowly fade-out the ground people. When you add a new factor into the training exercise, take steps back such as lowering the jumps or decreasing the distance between the points. Then, rebuild the other parts of the exercise back to the level before you added the new element. When you go somewhere new, go back to jumping very low fences and slowly build up the height. Taking these steps will help you have continued success and minimize the times your horse repeats the wrong behavior. Teaching him to jump in this manner maximizes his confidence, boldness, and relaxation.

As you approach bigger jumps, pay attention to both your horse's level of comfort and his jumping style. Does he tend to take off a distance away from the jump or does he prefer to jump from the base of the fence? Does he tend to spook at new jumps? Does he prefer jumping over wider jumps with two sets of standards (known as an oxer), or a narrow jump (a vertical)?

96-98 Vinton and I are teaching Hershey to free jump. He had been a very successful competitor, but he lost confidence when he was put up for sale and tried out by new riders. We needed to instill new trust in his own abilities. Vinton has pointed at me and said, "Go," and Hershey jumps toward me. As he commits and actually goes over the jump, I bridge. I reinforce him as soon as he reaches me.

99-101   Hershey's confidence is growing so we now put a rider (me) on his back. However, Vinton is directing the horse and I'm just "sitting there" using no aids so I don't confuse or worry Hershey. Vinton invites Hershey across the jump by calling his name and presenting the target to him.

In the beginning, bridge and reinforce all his good efforts but really reinforce him when he makes a decision that shows progress. For example, some horses are more comfortable leaving the ground further from the jump and may choose to stop if they get too close. When you see your horse choose to jump from the closer position and try to make the distance work out, make sure you strongly reinforce that decision. It shows he's trying harder than he did earlier in the process.

You may also choose to bridge the style of jumping you prefer, once your horse understands the fundamentals. If he is lazy with his hind end, for example, bridge and reinforce his jumping efforts only when he uses his hindquarters better. Remember to progress in small steps, building toward your goal. By allowing your horse to learn to navigate a course using On Target Training, he will develop into a more willing jumper.

BREEDING-SHED MANNERS

When it comes to breeding, the learning associations can be quite strong. Horses are born with the instinct to propagate to maintain their species. Breeding is a primary reinforcement, particularly for stallions. Mares sometimes seem somewhat intimidated by the process, but I wouldn't necessarily say reluctant.

In any case, what you have is much excitement on the part of both horses. Since horses are large and powerful, this can be a dangerous situation if things get out of control. This is another situation where you should seek professional advice if you are new to breeding.

I will offer some general guidelines, based on our On Target Training system. Let's talk first about mares. Before and after the breeding process, mares usually go through invasive veterinary procedures. I would therefore use a considerable amount of desensitization work to prepare for both the veterinary work and the process itself. (See Chapter Four.) Use the target to get her to stand quietly. Bridge and reinforce correct responses. Start this training well before the veterinarian arrives to expedite the exams and to keep everyone safe. When it comes time for breeding, bridge and reinforce as much as possible. Use the target to walk the mare to the breeding shed if she seems reluctant. (You may also walk her there several times between breedings to build a good reinforcement-history. This will teach her that every time she goes to the breeding shed does not result in an anxious situation.) Also, bridge and reinforce her for standing quietly.

Your goal is to keep her relaxed and calm until the stallion is presented. Then let nature take its course.

The stallion is usually more excited and less likely to listen to anything outside his sexual drive. There needs to be a balance here. You want him sexually driven but you also need him to listen and be responsive to you. Breeding is a primary reinforcement, but so is food. They are both very strong motivators. You should bridge-condition and target-train your stallion and teach him to lead with the hand-held target, wearing a halter and lead rope. He should learn to focus on the target. I would make this his strongest behavior. Before each meal I would have him touch the hand-held target with his nose and hold for a few seconds. Then build up the time. Make it very reinforcing for him to do this and be sure he does it regularly so it's not just associated with breeding.

I would, however, build up some specific association to breeding. Mary Shirley, a California breeder I know, has several breeding stallions. She told me she uses a specific halter for breeding that has a bell on it. When the stallion is breeding, he wears this halter. When he's not, he wears a regular halter. This is an excellent learning tool. We already know that horses learn through association. The stallion will hear the bell all through the breeding process. When there's no bell, he learns that there will be no breeding. Another popular association strategy is to lead the stallion out of the stall and turn one way for breeding, the other for different purposes. These techniques help reduce behavior problems between breedings. I also suggest bridging and reinforcing desired behavior. This will help teach your stallion to mind his manners and keep himself in check because he will gain the opportunity to get reinforced.

When it comes time to breed, you can make him aware of what will happen by using the halter bell and turning in a specific direction toward the breeding shed. At this point, he will understandably be anxious. Here, the target can come into play. Have him keep his nose on the target while he walks. When he does this relatively quietly, bridge and reinforce and keep walking. If he gets too excited, stop walking and reinforcing. This accomplishes two things: you have stopped reinforcing him with food and are not reinforcing him by getting closer to the breeding shed. When he is quiet, move forward again. If he gets too unruly, take him back to his stall. Try again in five minutes. Teach him he gets reinforced by food as well as by the breeding if he behaves well. Safety is the biggest issue here. If you teach him he can only breed when he minds his manners, you will see much improvement.

TEACHING A CONSTRUCTIVE BEHAVIOR TO REPLACE AN UNDESIRED BEHAVIOR

Teaching a constructive or alternative behavior to replace an undesired behavior is a useful tool in your repertoire. Technically, this is called "differential reinforcement of an incompatible behavior" or DRI. In terms of working with horses, it is defined as teaching a horse to perform a behavior that can't be achieved while performing an undesirable behavior. For example, your horse can't charge at you when you enter his stall if he's holding on a stationary target. By teaching him to hold on the target, you build a reinforcement-history with the stationary target. It will become more reinforcing for him to hold on the stationary target than it will be to charge at you. This way, you break the dangerous habit of charging by asking him to target before you enter his stall. We also use this technique when we begin bridge-conditioning. We teach horses to turn their heads away because this action is incompatible with trying to get at the food in our side-bucket.

This technique is illustrated throughout the book. Cibor's story from Chapter Five is one example. In his case, we taught him to move forward since moving forward was incompatible with the undesired behavior of ignoring the leg aids while working under saddle. We did this by making moving forward more reinforcing than his dull, reluctant way of going. Another example is teaching a horse to lower his head for clipping, which is incompatible with raising his head out of our reach. While walking to the paddock, holding on a target along the way is incompatible with bolting.

There are many applications for using this technique. Be creative. If you don't want your horse to run away with you while riding or longeing, make it more reinforcing for him to stop. Remember to set him up to succeed so you have the opportunity to build up a reinforcement-history with the new, more desirable behavior. DRI can be a very good tool for behavior modification and a constructive, kind method of eliminating unwanted behavior.

When implementing this technique, we need to keep in mind what we have already learned. First, identify the problem behavior and any contributing factors that may cause it to occur. Determine what the horse finds reinforcing about the behavior in question and then figure out what incompatible behavior you could substitute. Break it down into small steps and consider how you could set yourself and your horse up for success in this endeavor. Begin to work toward your goal. Remember to go slowly and be flexible. The idea is to rebalance the scales so your horse finds the new behavior more reinforcing than the previous one.

CHAPTER

Just for Fun!

e have found that most of the people who apply our On Target Training system to the serious side of horse training, such as solving difficult behavior problems or increasing athletic achievement, enjoy taking the process a step further and teaching their horses what can be considered "just-for-fun" behaviors. They've discovered that the benefits of teaching these behaviors are far more profound than might appear on the surface.

Most of the behaviors are fairly simple to learn and offer horses yet another way to earn the opportunity for reinforcement. Among the "just-for-fun" behaviors we teach are bows, leg-lifts, smiling, and head shaking. Our horses have shown us how much they enjoy this work. There have been times when we haven't worked with our horses for a few weeks. When we returned, they started soliciting our attention by offering their entire repertoire of behaviors. They weren't doing this because they were hungry. They'd been fed the same meals as usual, plus they were turned out on grass. They'd also had plenty of social interaction since we turned them out together all day. It was clear that they wanted to do the training sessions and interact with us. This type of reaction is not uncommon with animals trained through On Target Training. Horses want to interact with the people who train them.

Training these fun behaviors stimulates and challenges horses. Concurrently, responsiveness also increases. The more your horse knows, the sharper he becomes. Think of the mind as a muscle. The more it's used, the stronger it becomes. You can also help to minimize boredom and the neurotic behavior that stems from boredom. We are responsible for both the mental and physical well-being of our horses. People usually physically exercise their horses, but by interacting with them and giving them a challenge for their minds, we provide a different but equally worthwhile form of exercise.

Another benefit we discovered was a bit of a surprise. We found that working on one behavior improved others. When I thought about it, though, it made a lot of sense. By concentrating on correcting one undesired behavior, the horse's attitude about most other things improved as well, even though we didn't work on those things. By teaching horses a behavior such as targeting, other behaviors also became better.

I was surprised to learn this since the marine mammals at Sea World had been trained only with reward-reinforcement from the beginning of their interactions with people. Their attitudes were very upbeat and they seemed to thoroughly enjoy their jobs. Horses, however, may have experienced very different training techniques that led to less affirmative attitudes toward people or their training. They may not often have been given choices. On Target Training unlocks a cooperative attitude in horses who were previously resistant. Training horses to do fun behaviors improves their attitude across the board. Once we interact with them this way, they seem to perceive us a bit differently and enjoy being with us more.

HOW TO TRAIN "JUST-FOR-FUN" BEHAVIORS

As with all the work we do, begin by bridge-conditioning and target-training your horse. The target is an essential part of this type of training, so be sure your horse is adept at target work. I will outline the steps we have taken to teach some of these behaviors, but you may have great success devising your own approaches. Horses are individuals and think individually. If you took ten horses and taught them how to bow, the training method would be slightly different with each horse. With the bridge-signal and the target, you have all the tools you need to train your horse to do anything. Your imagination is your only limit, so don't be afraid to experiment and expand your boundaries.

Begin to use whichever stimulus you choose to be your horse's cue right away. It won't mean anything to your horse at first, but soon he will pair this cue with the actions that follow. He will see the cue and begin to anticipate what comes next.

• *The Bow*

First, think of the action you want to see and try to visualize what you can do to get your horse to do it. You will want your horse to keep his feet still—no walking—and you want him to stretch his head down to the ground. In order to lower his head all the way to the ground, he may need to move a leg out of the way. You'll also want to see his hindquarters shifting back over his hind feet. To begin, give the cue you decided upon for bowing. Then, ask him to lower his head by following the target down toward his chest. Next, move it lower toward the ground. Bridge and reinforce each effort when he follows the target without moving his feet. If he moves his feet, give him a three-second pause and repeat. Move the target a little less to allow him to grasp the concept of not moving his feet. If you see your horse start to shift his weight back, bridge and reinforce, since he will need to do this at some point to lower his head and shoulder toward the ground. Drawing attention to this step is good, even though it may come easily to your horse. Next, bring his head to the outside of one foreleg and down to the ground. Look for him to begin to move his leg out of the way of his head. He may start to kneel. Continue along this line until the behavior looks like what you had in mind. Then, begin to fade-out the target and watch for him to anticipate the behavior after you give the cue. Bridge and reinforce when you see him anticipate your request or the direction of the target: for instance, when he starts to swing his weight back and lower his head before the target gets there. This is progress. Strongly reinforce at this point (photos 102–104).

Start allowing a little more time between the cue and targeting to give your horse a chance to process his thoughts and time to anticipate the behavior. However, because he starts to anticipate where the target will be doesn't mean he's ready for the target to be eliminated. We are just beginning to fade-out the target. Let's say he lowers his head when he sees the cue. He still may need the target to help him follow through and shift his weight back. Repetition will help. If he gets frustrated, back up a step in the training process and get him back on the target. If he doesn't seem to be trying, end the session without reinforcing him. Come back in five or ten minutes and determine if his attitude is better. Most likely it will be. If not, try in a few hours or the next day.

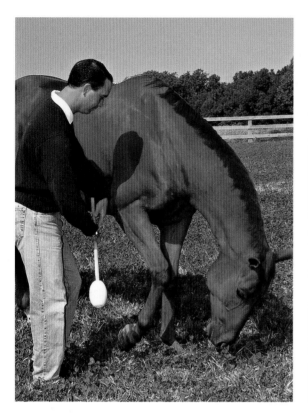 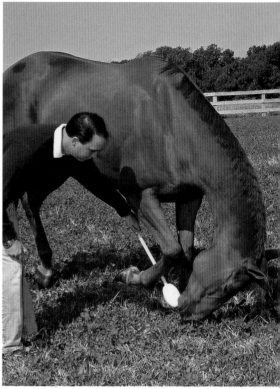

102-104 Teaching Mint to "bow." First, Vinton puts the target low between and behind Mint's legs. (If Mint walks back, Vinton will pause for three seconds to communicate that it is not what he wants). In the next photo Mint is getting his leg out of the way so he can touch the target. This is a good start to his rocking his weight back on to his hind legs so his back and shoulders can come lower to the ground. Remember that you should not attempt to teach this, or any other unusual behaviors, on anything but solid footing.

Check to be sure you are working on good footing. You'll have the most success on soft but stable ground. If it is cement or rocky, you'll have a harder time building his confidence. If the ground surface is grass, you may also have a more difficult time since grass could be a distraction. It will be easier to move to these more challenging surfaces after your horse has learned the behavior. Sometimes horses will paw the ground before lowering their heads. I don't mind this as long as it doesn't continue for a long period of time. When you first ask for a bow in a new area, take a

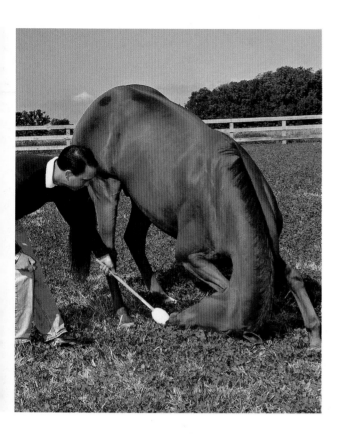

step back to help him focus. Then, progress forward again. It may take a week, or it may take a few weeks to train a bow. Patience and repetition will ensure your success.

• *Head Shake "Yes" and "No"*

Teaching your horse to shake his head "yes" and "no" requires the use of two targets. Use either hand-held targets or your hands as the targets. (It's easier to fade-out your hand when you use it as the target.) Before you begin, visualize the behavior you're going to teach. You would like to see your horse move his head up and down for "yes," or side to side for "no." He needs to stand still while he does his. Training the head shake "yes" and "no" is essentially the same process. However, we've found the head shake "yes" a natural, easy behavior to learn, while the head shake "no" seems to be more difficult and will take more time, repetition, and reinforcement. We'll focus on teaching the "yes" head shake.

Have two targets available. Begin by giving your horse a cue for the behavior. Use a high target to start him. As your horse reaches up to touch the target, bridge and reinforce. Then present another target lower down and bridge and reinforce when he touches this target. Repeat presenting both targets, looking for an up-and-down motion. Don't have him hold on them. Next, switch to using your hands as targets. Hold both hand targets up, presenting one and then the other. Starting at the top, present that hand in a deliberate manner. When he reaches toward it, bridge and then present the other hand target in a deliberate manner. When he moves toward that target, bridge and reinforce. Then look for him to move up and down between the targets again. Bridge the action you're looking for, but vary your bridges. Bridge some up movement and some down movement. Continue with this until he is doing the head shake "yes" (photos 105–107).

Next, its time to fade-out the targets. Start by eliminating the lower hand target. After this point, your bridges should come when he brings his head down. We want to communicate to him that this behavior is desired. Indeed, even though there is no longer a hand target being

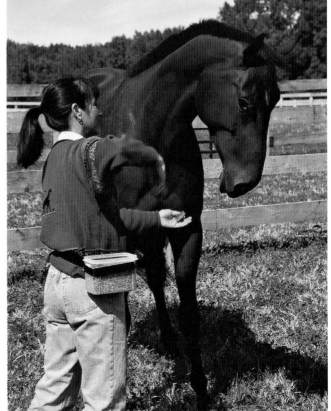

105-107   Here I'm teaching George to say "yes!" I use two hand-targets as cues, and bridge him when he goes down and when he goes up. You must remember to bridge the action you want to see repeated, which in this case, is moving his head both up and down.

108 Smiling! First, I touch Mint with my finger to get him to twitch his lip, then reward. Later, I gradually move this finger away and use it as the target while supporting Mint's chin with my right hand so he doesn't just poke his nose forward and out. Here he is successfully raising his lip toward my finger.

presented, use the bridge to draw attention to this healthy anticipation. If he has trouble, start again. When he is good at this, fade-out the upper hand target. He should now anticipate the desired behavior when you give the cue.

The head shake "no" is very similar to train but usually takes longer because it is more difficult for the horse. When we trained these behaviors, it took about a week to teach "yes" and about a month to teach "no." The time frame may vary for your horse but it shouldn't be a big issue. Focus instead on your horse's progress and his attitude.

• *The Smile*

This involves teaching your horse to lift his upper lip. For this behavior, I use my index finger for a target. Start by establishing a cue for the behavior. I have had the most success when I lightly support the horse's head with a hand under his jowl, about six inches back from his chin. This seems to help eliminate him wanting to reach out to my finger target. Support his head, then give the cue and touch his lip with your index finger. Look for the slightest movement from his lip. Bridge and reinforce. It may only be a slight twitch at first. In the beginning, you are teaching him to isolate and move his lips only. If he tries to open his teeth or nip, give him a three-second pause. Then, try again. Only bridge and reinforce movement from his upper lip. Continue until he lifts and holds his lip up. Fade-out your finger target gradually (photo 108).

109 Leg-crossing. We teach Mint to cross his front legs by manually placing his left leg across in front of his right leg, then bridging and reinforcing immediately. After a couple of times doing this, I cross my own legs in the same manner before going over to cross his again. He quickly learns that when I do it, I am going to ask him to do it too. Remember this sort of behavior, like all the others in this chapter, needs a great deal of reward-reinforcement.

These are just four examples of "just-for-fun" behaviors. There are many more you can train like spinning (you can review spinning on page 63), backing up (see page 42), and leg-crossing (photo 109): the list goes on. The target is instrumental in each of these lessons. For spinning, we utilize the target in quarter turns, progressing around in a circle. For backing up, we move the target back toward the horse's chest; as he tries to follow it, he backs up. Your only limit is your imagination.

When Vinton and I began training these behaviors, we made it up as we went along, using the bridge-signal and the target. With these essential tools at your disposal, you can train your horse to do whatever you wish, from fun behaviors to highly advanced work in any discipline. Indeed, once you get your horse on target, you can train your horse to do anything!

Glossary

Aversive An unpleasant or unwelcome stimulus (such as the application of bit pressure on the horse's mouth) often used in the process of removal-reinforcement. When the horse's response is correct, use of the aversive is discontinued.

Behaviors The particular actions or reactions of the horse to certain stimuli or his environment.

Bridge-Conditioning The process of pairing primary reinforcement with a bridge-signal in order to give the bridge-signal value.

Bridge-Signal A "yes" signal (the clicker, or other device) that communicates to your horse that he has performed the desired behavior. This signal bridges the time gap between the performance of correct behavior and the delivery of the reward-reinforcement. It also signals to the horse that he has completed a behavior to your satisfaction. For a new behavior, you will need to give him another cue.

Chain of Behaviors Step-by-step teaching of a succession of individual behaviors that will ultimately be performed in sequence. In riding, several actions, such as a canter depart, continuing the canter down the long side of the arena, collecting the stride, lengthening the stride, circling, and making a downward transition to the trot, are taught individually. The rider then gradually adds and links the separate elements until the horse can perform the entire chain together.

Classic Behavioral Conditioning The simple pairing of a stimulus with a reinforcement. For instance, in the case of Pavlov's dogs, it was the pairing of the sound of a bell with food.

Criterion/Criteria A standard or standards against which the performance of behaviors are measured.

Differential Reinforcement of Incompatible Behavior (DRI) A tool used to decrease undesired behavior by reinforcing a second behavior that is incompatible with the unwanted behavior. An example is reinforcing a horse for touching a target to replace his habit of charging toward you as you open his stall door.

Operant Conditioning This refers to the process of learning that certain actions or behavior get the horse what he desires, and that by repeating the behavior he will either get it or avoid it again.

Operant Performance An action or actions that change a horse's environment. A horse learns to operate on his environment via operant conditioning (see above) to gain things he desires.

Primary (Unconditioned) Reinforcer Something a horse needs to survive. One primary reinforcer is food.

Punishment Not to be confused with removal- or negative reinforcement. While both involve aversive stimuli, the difference is that removal-reinforcement is a highly effective training tool when used correctly. Punishment is not nearly as effective. Unlike removal-reinforcement, the animal has no way to stop punishment once it has started and it may cause the animal fear or anxiety. With removal-reinforcement, the animal can stop the aversive by stopping the undesired behavior.

Reinforcer Anything that increases the frequency of the behavior that precedes it.

Reinforcement-History An association that has been conditioned over time using particular stimuli including removal- and reward-reinforcement.

Removal-Reinforcement Discontinuing an aversive stimulus to reinforce a correct response, such as relieving bit pressure on a horse's mouth. A horse is reinforced for a correct response when the bit pressure is removed. Also known as negative reinforcement.

Reward-Reinforcer A pleasant or primary stimulus such as food that has a reinforcing value to a horse. Also known as a positive reinforcer.

Schedule of Reinforcement This refers to a pattern of delivery of reinforcement. An irregular pattern increases performance more than a predictable pattern of reinforcement.

Secondary (Conditioned) Reinforcer A stimulus, such as a clicker that becomes meaningful by pairing it with primary-reinforcement such as food.

Successive Approximations These are small step-by-step lessons building toward teaching new, sometimes complex, behaviors.

Superstitious Behavior An unintentional behavior (usually incorrect or unnecessary) that is accidentally reinforced.

Target A tool used to shape behavior, guide a horse through behaviors, and expedite the training process. There are different types of targets including stationary targets, hand-held targets, and the human hand. A target is a stick with an easily visible object such as a small white marine float on one end. A target can be affixed to a stationary object such as a wall, fence, or stall, or held in the trainer's hand. A hand target is the use of an open hand.

Target-Training The process of teaching a horse to touch, follow, or "hold" on a target with his nose.

Resources

For information on how to order On Target Training equipment, and to arrange clinics, seminars, demonstrations, or lectures, contact:

On Target™ Training
956 Glebe Road
Earleville, Maryland 21919-1306
phone: 800-638-2090 or 410-275-8141

Visit our web site at **www.on-target-training.com**

Video
YOU CAN TRAIN YOUR HORSE TO DO ANYTHING!: Clicker Training and Beyond

Photo Credits

Kelly Cannell
Pages 3, 4, 10

Jim Graham
Pages xviii, xix, 52, 93, 94, 114, 115, 149, 174, 175, 189, 191

Susan Karrasch
Pages xiv, 74, 75, 83, 86, 146, 147

Vinton Karrasch
Pages 130–133, 138–141

David Roberts, Roberts Photography
Pages 6, 15, 19, 28, 33, 42, 56, 61, 63–65, 103, 116, 117, 119, 121, 172, 176, 177, 184–187

Renie Poole, LK Photography
Pages 5, 7, 9, 22, 23, 40, 49, 54, 58, 59, 77–81, 88–90, 107, 108, 110, 111, 125, 127, 188

Index